McGRAW-HILL PROBLEMS SERIES IN GEOGRAPHY
Geographic Approaches to Current Problems:
the city, the environment, and regional development

Edward J. Taaffe, Series Editor

Wilfrid Bach
AIR POLLUTION

Kevin R. Cox
CONFLICT, POWER, AND POLITICS
IN THE CITY: A Geographic View

Richard L. Morrill and Ernest H. Wohlenberg
THE GEOGRAPHY OF POVERTY in the United States

Harold M. Rose
THE BLACK GHETTO: A Spatial Behavioral Perspective

David M. Smith
THE GEOGRAPHY OF SOCIAL WELL-BEING IN THE UNITED STATES:
An Introduction to Territorial Social Indicators

THE GEOGRAPHY OF
SOCIAL WELL-BEING
IN THE UNITED STATES

An Introduction to Territorial Social Indicators

DAVID M.SMITH

McGRAW-HILL BOOK COMPANY

New York   St. Louis   San Francisco   Düsseldorf   Johannesburg
Kuala Lumpur   London   Mexico   Montreal   New Delhi   Panama
Rio de Janiero   Singapore   Sydney   Toronto

Library of Congress Cataloging in Publication Data

Smith, David Marshall, 1936-
  The Geography of Social Well-being in the United States.

  Includes bibliographical references.
  1. U.S.—Social conditions—1960-
HN59.S58   309.1'73'092   72-6605
ISBN 0-07-058551-2   (pbk.)
ISBN 0-07-058550-4

The Geography of Social Well-being in the United States:
An Introduction to Territorial Social Indicators

1 2 3 4 5 6 7 8 9 0 DODO 7 9 8 7 6 5 4 3 2

This book was set in Baskerville by John T. Westlake Publishing
Services. The editor was Janis Yates; the designer was John T.
Westlake Publishing Services; and the production supervisor was
Sally Ellyson

The Printer and binder was R. R. Donnelley & Sons Company.

Because of our information gaps, national problems go nearly unnoticed until they suddenly are forced upon us by some significant development. Thus, we learn of widespread hunger in America, of the rapid deterioration of our environment, of dangerous tensions and unrest in our great urban centers, of the shocking conditions under which migrant farmworkers live, and of the absence of decent medical care for tens of millions of our citizens. We desperately need ways to monitor our social health and to identify such problems before they destroy our society.

Senator Walter Mondale, *Congressional Record,* January 25, 1971

. . .to do better, we must have a way of distinguishing better from worse.

Alice M. Rivlin, *Systematic Thinking for Social Action,* 1971

CONTENTS

EDITOR'S
INTRODUCTION

Whenever the question of the possible impact of social science on public policy is discussed, the need for social indicators is almost certain to be cited. One of the most exasperating features of the social sciences to date has been the absence of any agreed-upon set of measures of social conditions. We really have no way of knowing if things are getting better or worse in view of the bewildering diversity of standards of measurement attached to most social problems. Interest groups are relatively free to employ measures which support interpretations of social change designed to serve their own interests rather than to depict change accurately. Politicians may readily construct apparently objective indices to which the ins may point with pride but which the outs will view with alarm.

There is no question that social indicators are needed. The problem lies in agreeing on *which* social indicators would be most effective, and for what purposes. The author has carefully examined a wide variety of possible social indicators at different geographic scales, and presents here the pros and cons of several alternatives. He particularly stresses the need for geographic disaggregation. Aggregated national indicators obviously mask sharp contrasts between large regions such as Megalopolis and Appalachia in levels of social well-being; state indicators provide no distinctions between prosperous cities, declining cities, rich farmlands, and poverty-stricken areas of cutover forests and abandoned coal mines; metropolitan area indicators provide no basis for separating wealthy suburbs from inner-city pockets of poverty. In order to provide effective evaluation of welfare or anti-poverty programs, comparable measures must ultimately be available not only for an adequate time period, but also at a geographic scale appropriate to the conditions being treated, whether for an inner-city block, a group of low-income rural counties, or a large area such as the Upper Midwest.

Professor Smith has drawn upon on-going work in both geography and sociology. Both disciplines have dealt with city and regional classifications, social area analysis, and, more recently, factorial ecology. There is a regular progression from essentially intuitive classification schemes to objective but holistic statistical grouping procedures to the relatively objective but critically selective classification procedures associated with social indicators. The presence of such indicators, as Professor Smith points out, facilitates the next step: a realistic evaluation of the utility of public policies designed to bring us closer to achieving territorial social justice.

The Geography of Social Well-being is a logical companion volume to *The Geography of Poverty* by Richard L. Morrill and Ernest H. Wohlenberg. Professors Morrill and Wohlenberg select relatively few measures, primarily economic, and interpret their distribution in the United States. Professor Smith critically examines the strengths and weaknesses of the measures themselves, with emphasis on the need for moving beyond strictly economic criteria in the measurement of man's well-being.

EDWARD J. TAAFFE

PREFACE

The 1970s promise to be a decade of emerging social awareness in American geography. Traditional assumptions as to the nature and purpose of geographical inquiry are being challenged, and some restructuring of the subject as we know it can be expected. This will include the development of new ways of viewing the geography of national territories such as the United States, with more emphasis on the spatial expression of contemporary social problems.

Throughout the social sciences, there is a growing interest in the idea of "monitoring" the social state of the nation, in a similar manner to its economic state. This involves the development of sets of *social indicators,* to complement the existing economic indicators. But attention is generally focused on aggregate national conditions, rather than on the situation in different regions, cities and localities. Thus an important dimension of the social system is overlooked. To date, little attention has been given to the geography of social well-being in the United States, for geographers have been preoccupied with physical and economic conditions while most sociologists are not accustomed to thinking in spatial terms. The notion of *territorial social indicators*—the focus of this book—brings together certain substantive concerns of the sociologist and the distinctive perspective of the geographer.

The contemporary social indicators movement is an important reflection of changing criteria of "relevance," with respect to the activities of social scientists and the concerns of society at large. Yet it has attracted very little explicit attention in geographical circles, including those which emphasize social responsibility. This book attempts to relate the social indicators research of the past few years to the established approaches of geographical inquiry. The central thesis is that the development of territorial social indicators might provide a new conceptual and practical focus for human geography.

The approach adopted here is suggestive rather than definitive. It is a contribution to the current realignment of geographical research towards a direct confrontation with contemporary social problems. The content is conceptual rather than technical, though there is some discussion of measurement problems. The empirical material is very largely descriptive, for it would be unwise to try to explain what is as yet inadequately described. No rigorous interpretations of cause and effect relationships are offered, and no fresh solutions to contemporary problems are proposed. But the line of inquiry suggested in this book represents a necessary step in this direction—toward the design of a new and just society.

I am grateful to former colleagues associated with the Urban Studies Bureau, University of Florida, for providing the stimulating atmosphere of inter-disciplinary inquiry in which this project was completed. Their response to an early manuscript, together with that of some colleagues in the Department of Geography, was very helpful. Special acknowledgement is due to Professor Shannon McCune, Chairman of the Geography Department, and Professor Elizabeth Eddy, Director of the Urban Studies Bureau, for their encouragement and support of this line of research. A grant from the Social Sciences Council, University of Florida, facilitated the completion of an earlier report which formed the basis of this book, during the summer of 1971. The assistance of Mr. Ray Jones of the Research Library, and of Robert Gray, James Skinner and Steven Gladin (graduate students in the Department of Geography) was invaluable at various stages in the project. My gratitude to Margaret Smith is unlimited, for it was her professional concern for the socially deprived which first led me in the directions taken in this book, and it is her practical experience and sense of reality which keeps my feet somewhere near the ground.

DAVID M. SMITH

CHAPTER 1

GEOGRAPHY IN CONTEMPORARY SOCIETY

The social state of the nation is a matter of great concern in contemporary America. As in most other industrial nations, there is a long history of professional and philanthropic anxiety over the existence of social problems such as poverty, the conditions in the slums, and the decline of conventional morality. But recent years have seen an emerging popular interest, with daily mass-media discussions of environmental pollution, civil liberties, crime, drug addiction, and so on. Accompanying this is a growing expectation that the government will do more about these problems than simply issuing formal expressions of concern and offering ineffectual remedial programs. American society is changing, and new aspirations and priorities are taking shape.

Changing Social Priorities

The growing interest in social problems may be interpreted in part as a reaction to the materialism that has traditionally pervaded the American value system. It is gradually being appreciated that economic growth is a mixed blessing, and that Gross National Product and per capita income are not necessarily direct measures of the quality of life in its broadest sense. Never before has this society been better informed as to its shortcomings. And never before has any society been better placed, with respect to resources and skills, to deal with the less fortunate consequences of large-scale industrialization and urbanization. As Bauer (1968, 245-246) has remarked:

> The growing affluence of the society makes it possible, and to some extent imperative, to attend to phenomena which we once ignored. If technological growth creates structural unemployment, urban renewal and highway location displace people, industry and automobiles pollute the environment, it is no longer acceptable to shrug off these second-order consequences of our actions as "the price of progress."

1

Yet deeply-held values and old habits of mind are slow to change. The belief that the private production and consumption of goods and services and the endless advance of "technology" towards some unspecified objectives are the most important aspects of national life is still widespread. This belief is carefully fostered and reinforced by the economic interests that have most to lose by a change in attitudes, as they persuade us to consume material substitutes like cigarettes in place of real experience of the disappearing countryside, and to accept symbols like automobiles in place of the personal identity lost to many as they have become insignificant components in some gigantic production system.

The national government helps to perpetuate the existing value system by its emphasis on economic performance and technological gymnastics. National prestige is measured by success in the space race, the production of supersonic airplanes, and the conspicuous consumption of the material trappings of the affluent society. The monthly or annual figures on inflation, unemployment, or the value of production are announced with great solemnity and the shift of one percentage point can have major national political repercussions. Yet the figures for infant mortality and malnutrition are buried in statistical abstracts and seldom mentioned by Administration spokesmen, while the incidence of such conditions as heroin addiction, social alienation, and racial discrimination can be at best only informed guesses. National prestige in the social arena is more likely to come from heart transplants, and then from the number performed rather than the success rate, than from a general if undramatic increase in the overall level of health or welfare. It is only when it is realized and publicized that the United States has, for example, a worse level of infant mortality and life expectancy than more than a dozen other advanced industrial nations that real circumstances can be seen in perspective. And even then there is no guarantee that any serious attempt will be made to improve the situation.

The allocation of resources overtly reflects the priorities of a society. In the United States the proportion of the national budget spent on defense (and aggression), space exploration and the like, and the proportion of personal incomes spent on products such as automobiles, electric gadgets, and deodorants contrasts significantly with the meager appropriations for social programs and the regular defeat of local educational bond issues. The statement that follows (Terleckyj, 1970, B-776-77) puts it well by comparing social change with industrial innovation:

> *Social change is being produced by very backward industries.* Most of their products are not designed, they happen. Important issues in product mix, new product development, consumer research, industrial organization and pricing are being approached as a matter of course by faith and emotion, rather than by serious design. The science base for such social activities as education, design of living environments, welfare and most others, does not exist. . . . Compared to the care given, and properly given to, say, the design and operation of a commercial airliner or to the development and marketing of a new drug or even a cake mix . . . , the actual approaches in designing the schools our children go to, the neighborhoods we live in, or the manner in which we take care of our health are appallingly primitive.

And it is not just a case of government ineptitude against private business sophistication, as the strategy of the Department of Defense illustrates. As Rivlin (1971, 51) points out, "The problem of estimating the cost of alternative types of social action has not received nearly the attention that has been devoted to similar problems involving weapons systems." Very simply, it is a matter of priorities.

Clearly, a more effective approach to social planning and the design of social policy is needed. But this requires, in addition to changes in national values and priorities, masses of information that either do not exist or can be found only with great difficulty. Facts are needed desperately, to establish the state of the social system with respect to the incidence of conditions of concern, and to understand the way the system operates to produce these conditions. Only then can public intervention succeed in anything approaching a predictable manner.

Data on many aspects of society are missing or misleading, and there are no accurate yardsticks to indicate whether matters are getting better or worse. Governments in a number of countries are beginning to respond to the need for better social statistics, as is shown by the publication of *Toward a Social Report* (U.S. Department of Health, Education and Welfare, 1969) and the first issues of Britain's *Social Trends* (Central Statistical Office, 1970). There is also a growing interest within academic circles in the "monitoring" of the social system, in the development of "social indicators," and in the design of city and regional information systems for social planning. In short, there is a distinct shift away from economic affairs and towards more social matters, as the central national domestic area of concern.

This is the general context of the line of research developed in this book. It is concerned with geographical variations in social well-being in the United States, a matter that tends to be neglected in many contemporary discussions where the nation is viewed as a single entity. It represents an attempt to align geography with the social indicators movement, which may well be the most influential development in the social sciences in recent years.

Geography, Social Problems, and Social Justice

In social statistics, as in economic statistics, the emphasis has always been on the state of the nation as a whole. It is the national incidence of poverty and the national level of criminal activity that gets the attention in sociology and in the study of social problems, with regional levels mentioned only in passing, just as the economist talks of the national rate of unemployment and Gross *National* (not regional or city) Product. But it is becoming increasingly apparent that social problems, like economic problems, have an important spatial component, and that their incidence can be subject to extreme areal variations. The concentration of crime and other social pathologies in the inner city has been known and studied for years, and there can be few citizens who are not intuitively aware of extreme variations in risk to life and property from one neighborhood to another. The concentration of rural poverty and malnutrition in Appalachia and parts of the South was discovered in the 1960s, almost like a new continent or mountain range, and was given much publicity at the time. And interstate differences in welfare payments and services have been recognized as a major factor in the large-scale black migration from the South.

Geographical variations in social (and economic) conditions are thus very important indeed to the social state of the nation. Aggregate national statistics are, after all, a summation of the conditions of people differentiated by location of residence as well as in other respects. Aggregate statistics and national averages fail to show the local situations, and hence hide the extremes. Thus the national rate of infant mortality (1970) is 19.8 per 1000 live births (31.4 for non-whites), but it rises to 28.2 in Mississippi (over 40 for blacks) and drops to 14.1 in North Dakota. And within a city it can change from 100 to 10 in the few miles that separate the ghetto core from white middle-class suburbia. By this and many other social criteria large parts of the rural South and the inner areas of many American cities belong to the underdeveloped world, and not to the sophisticated modern industrial society that their inclusion in this nation's aggregate statistics implies.

The local and regional component can often be overlooked in the examination and interpretation of a national social problem. The United States' overall infant mortality figure is high when compared with most other modern industrial nations partly because of conditions in the ghettos and the South. If these areas were omitted from the national figure it would look much more respectable, and the United States might well lead the world. The figure in the high-mortality areas could clearly be reduced by public policy leading to the provision of basic ante- and post-natal medical care to which many people do not at present have access; yet in the United States the problem of infant deaths is perhaps more likely to be perceived as one requiring major innovations in medical science. Providing more doctors and medical care in Mississippi is almost certainly a more efficient (i.e., cheaper) way of reducing the national infant mortality rate than some expensive new machines in a private New York clinic. Failure to see this is, in part, the result of geographical ignorance.

Areal variations in social conditions are an important part of the national problem in an even more fundamental way. This relates to the concept of territorial social justice. It is axiomatic that a just society does not discriminate between individuals on the basis of race, color, or religion and if any such group is clearly differentiated from others with respect to the benefits and burdens society has to bestow, an unjust situation would be recognized. The case of the black population in the United States is the most obvious example. Geographical location is a characteristic of people in the same way as is race, color, and religion, yet it is very seldom that the question of areal or regional discrimination or inequality is brought up. When Mack (1970, 19) refers to "the need to correct inequalities in the educational opportunities available to Americans, regardless of race, color, and *region*" (emphasis added), the casual reader could well take "region" as a misprint for "religion" so rare is the use of the former term in this kind of context.

The concept of social justice is concerned with distribution and retribution—with the distribution of income broadly defined as "command over society's scarce resources" (Titmuss, 1962, 21-35) and other benefits, as they are allocated between different individuals and groups, and with the apportionment of burdens such as taxation and military service. The question of distribution (in a non-spatial sense) is of particular importance to social well-being (Winter *et al.,* 1968, 320):

> The general welfare of society is intimately related to the welfare or well-being of the individuals in it. The general welfare, however, is not simply the sum of the welfare of individuals. It is not necessarily promoted if, for example, the aggregate welfare increases because the rich get richer faster than the poor get poorer. The distribution of individual welfare, how many have how much (or how little), must be taken into account as well as how much there is overall.

The issue here is how to deal with the question of distribution when individuals are differentiated with respect to geographical location rather than (or as well as) by economic status, race, and so on.

Only one writer (Harvey, 1972) has attempted to examine social justice in spatial systems in a normative way. He reminds us that location analysis is heavily dependent on economic theory, and thus tends to rely on conventionally economic criteria of efficiency in passing judgement on the areal arrangement of phenomena. Yet there appear to be no logical reasons why the "social efficiency" or social justice of particular areal or regional distributions should not be considered.

The question of what comprises a just spatial distribution is a complex one, and need not be discussed in detail here. Establishing what it is that justifies an individual making claims on the product of a society involves moral judgements on the relative merits of the alternative criteria of need, work contribution, inherited rights, and so on, unless the principle of complete equality of claims is accepted. Harvey follows the ordering of Runciman (1966)—need, contribution to common good, and merit—and translates this into the notion that a just territorial distribution of income (broadly defined) would be such that (a) the needs of the people of each territory would be met, (b) resources are so allocated as to maximize inter-territorial multiplier effects thus rewarding contribution to the national economic good, and (c) extra resources are allocated to help overcome special difficulties stemming from the physical and social environment—which can be considered as cases of merit (Harvey, 1972,21). He also argues that, in a just distribution justly arrived at, the prospects of the least advantaged territory should be as great as possible. This suggests a spatial version of a commonly-held general approach to social justice, as expressed by Frakena (1962, 14) for example:

> A society is unjust if, by its actions, laws and mores, it unnecessarily impoverishes the lives of its members materially, aesthetically, or otherwise, by holding them at a level below that which some members at least might well attain by their own efforts.

There seems little doubt that there are many groups of people defined by their territory of residence that would fulfill these criteria of injustice.

It is obviously too early for any kind of rigorous assessment of the justice of particular areal distributions. However, some judgements can be made firmly if not definitively, and this process has in fact been going on for some time outside geography. By the criterion of need the lack of medical care facilities in some places is clearly unjust, as is the shortage of employment opportunities and the existence of substandard dwellings. A comparison between the ghetto and the suburbs in the American city is instructive: the disparity in the allocation of resources for social services is clearly unrelated to need; there are real questions as to whether suburbanites are over-rewarded in relation to their contribution to the general good when compared to the working poor of the inner city; and there is a reasonable argument for a merit payment to the productive resident in the difficult social environment of the ghetto. So the allocation of income and other benefits between these two territories is not only highly inequable but probably unjust by each of Harvey's three criteria. In fact, we should be suspicious of any situation in which the capacity of individuals to realize "the good life" (however perceived) varies markedly from place to place. Ultimately, any geographical pattern that reflects a distribution arrived at in a way that contravenes a society's generally accepted moral principles would be regarded *prima facie* as unjust.

Ideally, the basic objective of social policy is to identify the state of the social system and its subsystems, to compare this with some desired state that is both functional and conforms with accepted principles of social justice, and then to institute programs to correct the deficiency. But to do all this requires information (as well as much wisdom), which brings the discussion back to the starting point of this section. Identifying the geographical component in social problems is a necessary prerequisite to making the judgement as to how far the social state of the nation departs from the just ideal. It is not sufficient to show that black or Mexican Americans, for example, suffer disproportionately from poverty, that the poor experience various forms of social deprivation from which society's more affluent and influential members are protected, that certain religious minorities are discriminated against, and that there is a concentration of economic and political power in the hands of the wealthy. It is also necessary to establish how far people may be discriminated against on the basis of location alone, or how far their circumstances can be attributed to location in space rather than to race, color, or creed. This is where geography makes its most obvious contact with contemporary social concerns.

The Research Required

The shortage of adequate information on areal variations in social conditions has already been pointed out. It is partly an outcome of the failure to recognize the importance of the geographical component of national social problems, a subject that has unfortunately fallen between the two academic stools of geography and sociology. Geographers have traditonally ignored contemporary social problems almost completely, and sociologists, with the conspicuous exception of the Chicago ecological school and its followers (see Chapter 4), have generally given little attention to areal variations in the incidence of social conditions except for pointing out some broad regional differences and the concentration in the city slums. The geographer, who will draw maps of practically everything else, will seldom use this method to depict the distribution of social problems. And it is unusual to find a map in a sociologist's textbook.

These conditions seem to be changing, however. Geographers are becoming more socially aware, and sociologists perhaps a little more spatially aware. But there is some way to go yet before a satisfactory fusion of the two approaches takes place. The comparison with economic affairs is again instructive: considerable advances have been made in recent years in the fields of regional economics and regional science (largely the province of spatial economists), but despite the interest in urban sociology, it can hardly be claimed that there is yet a "regional sociology."

This book explores something of the borderland between geography and sociology. However, the approach is that of the geographer looking out from his own discipline, rather than that of someone with a foot firmly in both camps. In fact, despite the subject matter, this study is "pure geography" by most definitions of the field.

Our inquiry starts with the assumption that there is a dimension of human existence called social well-being, and that the people living in a specific area can be meaningfully differentiated from those living in other areas with respect to this dimension and its various component parts. Exactly what is meant by social well-being is the subject of discussion in Chapter 6. It is sufficient here to say that it relates to income in its broadest sense, physical health, and state of mind—three basic conditions of individual well-being recognized in the literature for many years (e.g., Bossard, 1927). The concept of social well-being comes close to that of "the quality of life," and to some writers they appear synonymous. If there is a significant difference, it is probably because criteria of social well-being depend less on subjective judgement and on the varying perceptions of individuals than does the nature of the good life. The concept of "happiness" would represent a still higher order of abstraction. As Rossi points out, "Happiness is too personal and subjective a phenomena to be studied by the crude measuring devices presently available to the social scientist" (Bradburn and Caplovitz, 1965, v), but the concept of social well-being can be made operational, albeit with difficulty, despite the present shortage of suitable models and measures.

The research to be presented is almost entirely descriptive in nature. The general working hypothesis is that social well-being in the United States is subject to measurable differences from place to place and to fairly regular spatial variations. The task is to establish an operational definition of social well-being, to compile the data necessary to determine the degree and regularity of spatial variations, and to set down these observations in numerical and cartographic form. The end result should be a set of "territorial social indicators." The practical contribution is implicit in the discussion in the previous section: an accurate description of the geography of the social state of the nation is a necessary preliminary to the understanding of the structure and performance of the social system required for the development of sensible national social policy. The results should also be of educative value, providing information on the basic social geography of the nation for students (and citizens) at present kept largely ignorant of these matters by the economic value bias of existing literature.

In a geographical inquiry of this kind the choice of the spatial scale at which to operate is invariably a critical question. This work will focus its investigations at three different levels for which data are available or can be compiled—inter-state, inter-city, and intra-city. Whatever the level, it must be understood that data on any particular territory are aggregates of individual experience, just as they are at a national level. All the well-known dangers of ecological social research will be present. There will also be a temptation to read too much into location as an independent variable in spatial differences in social well-being. It is easy to forget that per capita income in a southern city may be low because of the predominance of a particular racial group whose income is generally low irrespective of location, rather than because the city is southern. However, southern blacks may be worse (or better) off than northern blacks. Attempting to unravel some of the interconnections between the level of social well-being, its basic causes, and geographical location should be a central objective of the line of inquiry initiated in this book.

The discussion continues with overviews of the literature concerned with spatial variations in social conditions within the United States. Chapters on the regional approach (Chap. 2), city classification (Chap. 3), and urban social ecology (Chap. 4) correspond with the three spatial scales at which this inquiry is being conducted. Then follows a review of the "social indicators movement"—the academic and governmental expression of current concern over the inadequacy of social statistics and the management of social policy (Chap. 5), which leads to discussion of territorial social indicators and the selection of criteria of social well-being (Chap. 6). A summary of the results of some preliminary attempts to construct territorial social indicators at the inter-state, inter-city and intra-city levels follows (Chapters 7, 8, and 9). The book concludes with an examination of some of the problems and prospects of this line of research, as it related to public policy (Chap. 10).

REFERENCES CITED

Bauer, R. A. (1968), "Social Indicators: Or Working in a Society Which has Better Social Statistics," in S. Anderson, ed., *Planning for Diversity and Choice*, MIT Press, Cambridge, Mass., pp. 237-250.

Boskoff, A. (1970), *The Sociology of Urban Regions*, Appleton-Century-Crofts, New York.

Bossard, J. H. S. (1927), *Problems of Social Well-Being*, Harper & Brothers, New York and London.

Bradburn, M. N. and Caplovitz, D (1965), *Reports on Happiness—A Pilot Study of Behavior Related to Mental Health*, Aldine, Chicago.

Central Statistical Office (1970), *Social Trends*, No. 1, Her Majesty's Stationery Office, London.

Frankena, W. K. (1962), "The Concept of Social Justice," in R. B. Brandt, ed., *Social Justice*, Prentive-Hall, Englewood Cliffs, N.J., pp. 1-29.

Harvey, D. (1972), "Social Justice in Spatial Systems," in R. Peet, ed., *Geographical Perspectives on American Poverty*, Antipode Monographs in Social Geography, No. 1, Worcester, Mass., pp. 87-106.

Mack, R. W. (1970), "Is the White Southerner Ready for Equality?," in Mack, ed., *The Changing South*, Aldine, Chicago, pp. 9-20.

Rivlin, A. M. (1971), *Systematic Thinking for Social Action*, The Brookings Institution, Washington, D.C.

Runciman, W. G. (1966), *Relative Deprivation and Social Justice*, Routledge and Kegan Paul, London.

Terleckyj, N. E. (1970), "Measuring Progress towards Social Goals: Some Possibilities at National and Local Levels," *Management Science*, 16, pp. B-765-778.

Titmuss, R. (1962), *Income Distribution and Social Change*, Allen and Unwin, London.

U.S. Department of Health, Education and Welfare (1969), *Toward a Social Report*, USGPO, Washington, D.C. and Ann Arbor Paperbacks, University of Michigan Press, 1970.

Winter, J. A., *et al*, ed. (1968), *Vital Problems for American Society: Meanings and Means*, Random House, New York.

CHAPTER 2

AREAL CLASSIFICATION AND THE REGIONAL APPROACH

Geography is variously defined as the science concerned with spatial organization, location analysis, man-environment relationships, or areal differentiation. Geographers are professionally interested in how and why one piece of territory differs from another with respect to both its physical (natural) environment and the activities of man. The classification of the earth's surface through the identification of regions of relatively homogeneous character or functional cohesion is central to geographical method. Such classification is the way in which geographers conventionally summarize the complexity of the world as they observe it from their spatial perspective.

Social Conditions in Geographical Research

A critical question in geography is the selection of the phenomena or variables significant to the study of areal differentiation, or the criteria for regional identification and delineation. For a long time the focus was on the natural environmental factors of relief, climate, vegetation, and so on. It was assumed and demonstrated, fallaciously for the most part, that areal differences with respect to human activity tended to mirror the natural or physical regional structure, an approach generally described as environmental determinism. Today there is more emphasis on economic regions, characterized by some particular concentration or combination of productive activity, and on the study of the way man behaves in organizing his life on the surface of the earth. However, geography has not yet reached the point at which regional social character and structure is recognized as a major element in the areal differentiation of national territories in the advanced industrial world, despite the cultural geographer's interest in these aspects of more primitive societies.

Until very recently geographers showed little professional interest in contemporary social problems. Responding to the prevailing values of society, they have been far more concerned with studying the production of goods and the exploitation of resources than with the conditions in which people live. There is a branch of the subject termed Social Geography but little progress has been made in this field unless it is defined narrowly enough to exclude such matters as poverty, hunger, medical care, welfare services, drug abuse, crime, and other social pathologies. One purpose of this book is to attempt to correct this serious bias in the geographer's view of the world in general and of this nation in particular.

The lack of geographical concern with social conditions can be confirmed by a cursory glance at the literature. If social well-being relates to such things as material living standards, health, education, welfare, and the incidence of social pathologies, then this is a subject that has been almost entirely neglected. A review of the contents of the textbooks and atlases dealing with the United States will illustrate this point and the professional journals give a similar impression.

However, there are some recent indications of change. This is exemplified by scholarly papers on such topics as the ghetto (e.g., Morrill, 1965; Rose, 1970), poverty and hunger in America (Thompson, 1964; Morrill, 1969; Peet, 1971), socio-economic well-being in Mississippi (Lowry, 1970), and crime in America (Harries, 1971). The periodical *Antipode: A Radical Journal of Geography* provides a forceful expression of this growing social awareness. The first impact in book form is represented by the present series, which began with studies of the geography of poverty (Morrill and Wohlenberg, 1971) and the black ghetto (Rose, 1971).

The circumstances that have allowed or encouraged the geographer's neglect of social problems need not be considered here. It is sufficient to attribute it to academic inertia and to a degree of caution in the choice of subject matter for classroom and textbook that may represent, in part, a reluctance to become involved in political issues. There are some signs of a fundamental change in these attitudes, however, with the emergence within the geographical profession of a new movement calling for increased professional social responsibility (see Smith, 1971).

Multivariate Regionalization

One of the perpetual problems in a regional analysis in geography is the necessity of considering simultaneously a number of diverse conditions or variables. This may help to explain the exclusion of the incidence of social problems in regional schemes, where consideration of employment structure alone once pushed the geographer's analytical techniques to the limit. But at the end of the 1950s geography discovered factor analysis.* The

* Factor analysis and principal components analysis have figured prominently in geographical research in recent years. These techniques are generally used to extract the "underlying" or "basic" dimensions of variance within large matrices of numerical data, by deriving a relatively small number of composite variables (factors or

capacity of this technique to extract the basic dimensions of variance from data on the areal incidence of large numbers of conditions gave the geographer a powerful new tool which he was quick to apply to areal classification and the identification of regions. It has also been used at the inter-city and intra-city levels as will be shown in subsequent chapters of this book.

At the regional level, most applications of this multifactor regionalization approach have been concerned with the analysis of spatial variations in "economic health." This started with a study of New York State by Thompson *et al.* (1962), and has subsequently been attempted elsewhere in the United States, in Canada (e.g., Bell and Stevenson, 1964; Berry, 1965), in Britain (Smith, 1968), and in a number of other countries. The procedure is to select a number of different criteria of economic health (well-being, or progress) such as income, employment levels, demographic trends, industrial production and economic growth, apply factor analysis or principal components analysis (R-mode) to the intercorrelation matrix derived from areal values for these variables, and use the factor scores as territorial indices of economic health.

Paradoxically, the main danger with this method of approach exists in the very ease with which it can be applied. Computer programs are readily

components) accounting for a relatively large share of the original information. This is possible because many individual variables are quite highly intercorrelated, thus differentiating between areas in a similar manner. The territorial units of observation can be given scores on these composite variables.

Both techniques begin with a matrix of dimensions $m \times n$, where m is the number of variables and n the units (territories) of observation. The data are transformed into Z-scores, and an intercorrelation matrix $(m \times m)$ is calculated. The solutions of a factor analysis and a components analysis then differ slightly. Principal components analysis begins with an intercorrelation matrix with values of unity in the principal diagonal, and generally performs an orthogonal transformation of the original m variables into a new set of the same number. All the variance in the original matrix is accounted for by the new variables, or components. Factor analysis begins with an intercorrelation matrix which can have values of less than unity in the principal diagonal. This model generally involves a prior hypothesis as to the number of underlying factors. The number of factors extracted is less than the number of the original variables, and some residual variance will be accounted for by an error term. The choice between a factor or components model depends upon the nature of the research problem.

Each factor or component is identified by a set of "loadings," which measure the simple correlation (r) between the new composite variable and each of the original variables. The high-loading variables are used to give a name to the new variable, indicating the general conditions which it reflects most closely. The leading components or factors will account for relatively large shares of the variance in the original data matrix. Territorial scores on the composite variables are derived basically by multiplying the original values (Z-scores) on each variable by the appropriate loading. Scores on the leading factors or components derived from a set of data relating to social conditions thus provide effective general territorial social indicators.

Further particulars of the computational procedures, and some of the problems in factor analysis or principal components analysis, may be found in specialized texts and papers, some of which are listed in the references at the end of this chapter (Guertin and Bailey, 1970; Harman, 1966; King, 1969; Rummel, 1967.)

available, and the mathematics can be performed in a few seconds for a few dollars. The census and other official statistical abstracts can be found on most library shelves and it is a simple matter to extract data by states or by a group of counties on dozens of different variables that appear to have a bearing on the rather imprecise notion of economic health. This kind of multifactor regionalization has thus been used indiscriminately at times, with the numerical inputs determined by the content of the census rather than by logical derivation from some conceptual framework. To find information on variables not in the census or other easily obtained source often requires more time and effort than a researcher is prepared to give the project.

As a consequence of all this, the studies in multifactor regionalization have remained largely economic in their selection of criteria. In most of them social health or well-being is covered only via income, and by such figures on length of education and quality of housing as are included in the census. It is extremely unusual to find social conditions like infant mortality and physical health included, and if they are included they are greatly outnumbered by more conventional economic variables. Such an approach may, of course, be justified on the grounds that social well-being is likely to be relatively highly correlated with economic health, but it is unfortunate that more social variables have not been included and that multifactor regionalization has not been extended to the concept of social health.

It is perhaps surprising, in view of the popularity of this technique, that there are very few published attempts to replace the conventional regional subdivisions of the United States by a system based on a multitude of different criteria. One analysis that attempted to reflect a wide range of geographical phenomena, including social conditions, was performed by Cole and Smith (1967; Cole and King, 1968, 295-304). They selected twenty-five variables by states, ranging from physical conditions to political affiliation, and including in the social realm persons per lawyer, school years completed, expenditures on education, physicians per capita, infant mortality, and housing quality as well as income and measures of material affluence. The first factor, accounting for 35 percent of the total variance, is clearly related to what might be termed socio-economic well-being. It loads heavily on housing, the telephones to population ratio, income, physicians, urban population, and school expenditures, in that order. The highest five state scores on this factor (i.e., the "best" states) are New York, Connecticut, New Jersey, California and Massachusetts, while the lowest five are (from the bottom) Mississippi, South Carolina, Alabama, Arkansas and North Carolina. Insofar as scores on this factor comprise a possible index of relative state socio-economic well-being, there are fairly clear regional differences, with the "best" states concentrated in the major manufacturing belt from Illinois to Massachusetts and in the West, while the "worst" comprise a solid block of ten southern states together with the Dakotas. It is significant that this interesting study is reported in print in a book on techniques rather than in a text on the United States.

Towards a Regional Geography of Social Well-being

The geographer has powerful techniques at his disposal for analyzing spatial variations in a large number of different conditions simultaneously. Now he needs the inclination to study social problems with the thoroughness he has hitherto devoted to examining physical and economic phenomena. There is no lack of justification, for if geography is what geographers say it is there are sound reasons for the study of many social variables that have previously been largely ignored.

If geography is concerned with areal differentiation and the identification of regions, then the incidence of social problems might be highly relevant criteria. For example, if the intra-city or inter-regional levels of social deprivation were depicted as three-dimensional surfaces representing poverty, health, education, and so on, their topography might be just as dramatic as the physical and economic surfaces to which we attach so much importance. If geography has to do with location analysis and spatial organization, then the location of social service facilities such as hospitals in relation to the needs of the client population might be just as significant as the location of retail outlets and the arrangement of their market areas. If geography is interested in the spatial coincidence of phenomena and their possible causal relationships, then there is much in the realm of social problems to excite our curiosity. Examples would be the coincidence of racial discrimination, poverty, malnutrition, and ill health in parts of the rural South, and the concentration of social pathologies in the inner city.

Thus on the grounds of simple logic, the conventional definitions of geography seem to require consideration of a wide range of social conditions that have traditionally been ignored. When the growing public concern about social problems is added, the case seems unassailable. Geography is now emerging from its quantitative and model-building revolution with more effective tools and better research design than it had before; what is now needed is a critical review of the scope and philosophy of the subject. Geography appears to have been so tightly locked into traditional ways of structuring knowledge, so deeply committed to existing paradigms, and recently so preoccupied with techniques and methodology that it has tended to overlook the growing disparity between its subject matter and the changing concerns of society at large (Smith, 1971, 156). It is time for a humane human geography.

As geography redefines its scope and purpose against new criteria of social relevance, the kind of variables examined can be expected to change. But what will be the new concepts upon which the geographer will attempt to structure his observations concerning areal differentiation? What are the additions or alternatives to such concepts as "man-land relationships," "economic character," and "economic health" which have to such a marked degree determined the conditions which geographers have investigated in recent years? The central thesis of this book is that "social well-being" is such a concept.

Discussion of the meaning of social well-being is reserved for later chapters, following the coverage of certain necessary groundwork. But possible lines of geographical inquiry at the regional level which relate to this concept can be identified in the existing literature. Some of these are illustrated in the remainder of this chapter.

Community "Efficiency" and Levels of Living

One obvious innovation would be to include more social variables in the kind of studies of areal differentiation which are often performed on county census data. An instructive example is provided by a study of the state of Ohio (Munson, 1968). The purpose of this research was to determine the underlying structural order of communities defined as "a relatively self-sufficient population, residing in a limited geographical area, bounded together by feelings of unity and interdependency in meeting man's basic social and biological needs" (Munson, 1968, 5). The county was taken as the unit of observation, and data were compiled on 113 variables suggested by the concept of community quoted above.

The variables selected were predominantly the demographic, occupational, and economic features usually included in geographical economic-health studies. But they also included such social problem conditions as illiteracy, accidental deaths, morbidity, poverty, income distribution, crime and juvenile delinquency, mental illness, suicide, alcoholism, venereal disease, divorce, illegitimacy, and welfare dependence. Data on these conditions are not included in the census, and had to be compiled from the records of local government agencies.

Table 2.1. The Composition of Munson's Community Efficiency Index for Ohio counties

1. *Dwelling Condition*
   a) Percent of housing units, 1960, "sound with all plumbing facilities"

2. *Health Index*
   b) Infant deaths per 1000 live births, 1960
   c) Deaths from all causes per 1000 population, 1960
   d) Tuberculosis deaths per 100,000 population, 1960

3. *Social Control*
   e) A crime index derived by the following formula:
      Crime = 4 (Criminal Homicide Rate) + 2 (Robbery Rate) +
      1 (Burglary Rate), where rates are based on convictions per
      100,000 population
   f) Number adjudged to be delinquent per 1000 persons in school, aged 7-17

4. *Welfare*
   g) Percent of families, 1960, having incomes of less than $3,000 in 1959
   h) Per capita expenditure on "Aid to Dependent Children," 1960
   i) Percent of total "Aid to Dependent Children," 1960
   j) Per capita expenditure for "General Relief," 1960

The Index is derived by summing the ranks for the lettered variables grouped under each heading, re-ranking, and then summing the four sets of ranks on the numbered criteria. The result is an index number for each county.
Source: Munson (1968, 15).

The completed data matrix was subjected to factor analysis, and seven leading factors were identified. These were : I - Urbanism, II - Level of Living, III - Population Growth, IV - Agricultural Productivity, V - Social Control, VI - Taxable Wealth, and VII - Insured Labor Force. The factor structures revealed some interesting relationships with social problem conditions. For example, the loadings on the Urbanism factor showed correlations of .90 with alcoholism, .78 with venereal disease, and .63 with illegitimacy, supporting the often-proposed association between city life and social disorganization. The Level of Living factor correlated —.69 with technical illiteracy, showing the inverse association between poverty and education.

From the results of the factor analysis, Munson developed standard county profiles with respect to performance on each factor. Then scores were given to each county, showing the extent of its departures from the standard. When these county scores were mapped for the leading factors considerable geographical regularity appeared, differentiating the north-western half of the state from the southeastern half. Thus important regional variations in community structure were revealed.

A particularly interesting inclusion in Munson's analysis is a variable described as "Community Efficiency." This is a combined index derived by adding the reversed ranks achieved by counties on a broad range of social conditions representing housing, health, crime and poverty (see Table 2.1). The values of this Community Efficiency Index are mapped in

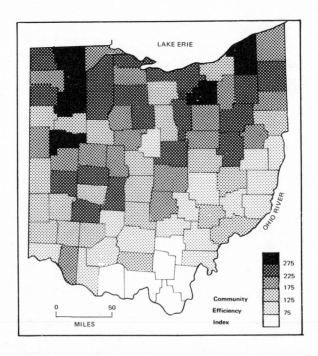

Figure 2.1 Community Efficiency Index for Ohio Counties, 1960. (Source of data: Munson, 1968, 224.)

Figure 2.1. This shows quite a clear differentiation of the state, with a solid southeastern region of low community efficiency, a northern region of generally high indices, and a discontinuous transitional zone between them.

Another interesting study at the county level is that of Lewis (1968) on the northeastern United States. He developed "level-of-living" indices from twelve variables relating to population migration, education, employment status, housing, telephones, political participation, health, and family stability. These were mapped and used in the delineation of level-of-living regions—an approach that could be applied nationally to good advantage.

The Regional Geography of Poverty

At the beginning of the 1960s America discovered poverty on a scale hitherto unimagined. Much of the credit for arousing the initial popular concern went to Michael Harrington (1962), who wrote of the "other America" largely unknown to the affluent majority. As government responded lack of sound information was a major problem so poverty became an important research topic.

Various attempts were made to measure the nature and extent of local poverty in the United States. One was in the series of *Community Profiles* developed by the Office of Economic Opportunity in order to provide information to support the planning and evaluation of programs for community improvement. For each of 3135 counties, data were compiled on twelve "poverty indicators" (Table 2.2). This information was used to

Table 2.2. *Poverty Indicators used in the Office of Economic Opportunity community profiles*

1.	*Magnitude of Poverty:* number of families with incomes below Social Security Administration poverty cutoff, 1966
2.	*Severity of Poverty:* percent of families with incomes below Social Security Administration poverty cutoff, 1966
3.	*Economic Compensation:* average first quarter gross earnings for employees in all industries, 1964
4.	*Economic Activity:* retail sales per person, 1966
5.	*Family Resources:* median family income, 1966
6.	*Employment Conditions:* percent of labor force unemployed, 1960
7.	*Educational Achievement:* median school years completed by persons age 25 and over, 1960
8.	*Functional Illiteracy:* percent of population failing to complete over four years of school, 1960
9.	*Adequacy of Health Care:* physicians per 100,000 population, 1962
10.	*Health Status:* infant deaths per 1000 live births, 1964
11.	*Sufficiency of Housing:* percent of dwelling units with more than 1.01 persons per room, 1960
12.	*Agricultural Prosperity:* value of farmer level-of-living index, 1960

Source: U.S. Department of Commerce, Bureau of Standards (1969, 4-5).

determine the "normal or typical" level of each indicator, represented by the value for the median county. Then the relative performance of each county (community) could be found for each poverty indicator. The profiles were printed out by computer in graphic form. An example, for Hillsborough County in Florida (including the City of Tampa), is illustrated in Figure 2.2. The horizontal bars show the extent to which the county performance is unfavorable or favorable, compared with the national norm.

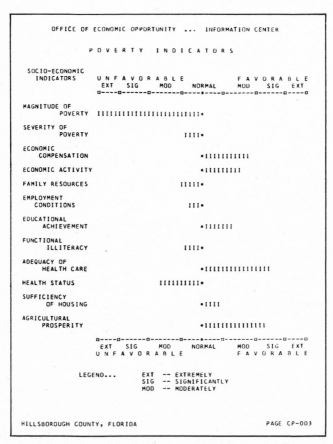

Figure 2.2 Community Profile for Hillsborough County, Florida, based on twelve poverty indicators. (Source: U.S. Department of Commerce, National Bureau of Standards, 1969, 003.)

Information such as this, updated and with other variables added, could easily be used to develop alternative national regional subdivisions to those based on physical and economic conditions which dominate the textbooks. An important start has been made in an earlier book in this series (Morrill and Wohlenberg, 1971, 103-117) with the identification of poverty regions of the United States bas   on data for State Economic

Areas. As the focus on poverty is extended into a concern for the broader concept of social deprivation, a new regional geography of social well-being should emerge.

An Inter-state Study of the "Quality of Life"

The most ambitious attempt thus far to measure inter-regional and inter-state variations in social well-being has come from an economist (Wilson, 1969) and not from a geographer. Wilson argues that even with the existing sources of data it is possible to construct a number of social indicators that provide a much broader measure of inter-regional differences in social well-being (social welfare, or the quality of life) than is currently available. He selected nine of the eleven "domestic goal areas" included in the report of the President's Commission on National Goals (1960)—Status of the Individual, Equality, Democratic Process, Education, Economic Growth, Technological Change, Agriculture, Living Conditions, and Health and Welfare; those not included were Arts and Science, and Democratic Economy. His aim was to measure the relative position of each of the states in these nine general areas.

Wilson proceeded as follows. He selected eighty-five different variables relating to the nine goal areas, and used them to produce nine summary indicators. The Status of the Individual was measured by levels of public assistance, quality of medical services, education, and equality. Individual Equality was measured by white/non-white ratios on such conditions as unemployment, income, education, health, and housing quality. State and local government (i.e., Democratic Process) evaluations were by measures of citizen participation and information levels, the professionalism of public administration and state legislatures, and the state/local dispersion of power. Education was measured by various achievement and enrollment levels. Economic Growth was measured by increases in income, and by capital outlays and other input conditions. Technological Change was measured by patents issued, research expenditures, research manpower, and vocational education levels. Agriculture was measured by the farm level-of-living index, and the value and attributes of farms. Living Conditions were represented by spending levels on anti-poverty programs, housing quality, crime, the extent of inner-city concentration of the poor, and recreational areas. Health and Welfare was measured by health facilities available, hospital admissions, infant mortality, welfare expenditures, and so on. The complete list of variables and their sources will be found in Wilson (1969, 35-43).

Factor analysis was used to reduce the initial sets of observations on the variables relating to each goal area to an aggregate score. For each of the nine goals, scores on the leading factor extracted were used to rank the states (Table 2.3). Although state ranks on the nine separate goals are generally quite similar there are some interesting differences. For example, California ranks first in Individual Status, Education, and Technological Change, but only fourteenth in Health and Welfare; Minnesota ranks first in Health and Welfare but only seventeenth in Education.

Table 2.3. Wilson's analysis of "Quality of Life" in the United States: individual state rankings for the nine social indicators, 1960-1966

	Individual Status	Racial Equality*	State & local gov- ernment	Educa- tion	Economic growth quality	Techno- logical change	Agricul- ture	Living condi- tion	Health and welfare
Alabama	47	34	34	49	38	21	48	47	45.5
Alaska	32	19	20	37	47	49	35.5	26	25
Arizona	30	23	21	5.5	27	28	1	31	39
Arkansas	46	37.5	48	44	42	35	49	41	36
California	1	3	4	1	3	1	2	3	14
Colorado	13	2	17	18.5	16.5	19	8.5	24	6
Connecticut	4	11	3	4	7	14	8.5	1	9
Delaware	27	28	16	21	4	29	12.5	8	3
Florida	29	35.5	18	36	15	7	34	37	43
Georgia	48	35.5	40.5	46	22	24	41	45	40
Hawaii	22	1	2	35	13	40	15	7	27
Idaho	24	–	36	9	25	43	12.5	18	45.5
Illinois	5	15	8	8	5	10	7	14	21
Indiana	23	12.5	27	13.5	12	17	17.5	34	37.5
Iowa	15	6	31	23	10	26	4	29	13
Kansas	20	15	29	12	30	31	17.5	38.5	34
Kentucky	40	26	50	40	24	30	45	27	47
Louisiana	41	32	38	41	41	25	40	49	31
Maine	36	–	23	45	49	50	37	15	23
Maryland	26	25	13.5	18.5	2	15	21.5	21	5
Massachusetts	3	7	1	2	18	4	27.5	9	12
Michigan	10	10	12	16	1	8	31	13	42
Minnesota	9	4	7	17	6	11.5	21.5	10	1
Mississippi	50	39	45	47	35	38	50	46	48
Missouri	38	20	35	28	39	20	38	36	28
Montana	19	–	37	25	46	47	5.5	23	19
Nebraska	31	21.5	33	10	23	39	10.5	40	29
Nevada	18	–	26	31	26	44	8	5	35
New Hampshire	16	–	32	33	33.5	42	32	19	22
New Jersey	6	18	6	5.5	19	9	10.5	4	24
New Mexico	39	24	43	32	48	36	35.5	32	44
New York	2	12.5	5	3	16.5	2	19	2	2
North Carolina	45	33	28	48	32	18	43.5	44	33
North Dakota	28	–	40.5	27	20	41	21.5	33	8
Ohio	14	17	15	29	29	6	25	17	30
Oklahoma	34	27	42	20	45	23	39	43	17
Oregon	12	8	11	13.5	8	32	16	11	11
Pennsylvania	17	15	9.5	24	40	5	29.5	16	16
Rhode Island	7	–	13.5	11	31	37	25	6	4
South Carolina	49	40	30	50	37	33	43.5	48	50
South Dakota	37	37.5	47	26	44	48	21.5	35	18
Tennessee	44	30	44	42	21	22	46	38.5	37.5
Texas	43	29	25	34	33.5	3	33	50	49
Utah	21	1	22	7	28	27	25	20	41
Vermont	33	–	24	38	36	45	29.5	25	10
Virginia	42	31	39	39	9	16	42	42	26
Washington	11	5	19	15	14	13	14	12	20
West Virginia	35	21.5	49	43	50	34	47	30	15
Wisconsin	8	9	9.5	30	11	11.5	27.5	22	7
Wyoming	25	–	46	22	43	46	5.5	28	32

*Data available for only 41 states.

Source: Wilson (1969, 13).

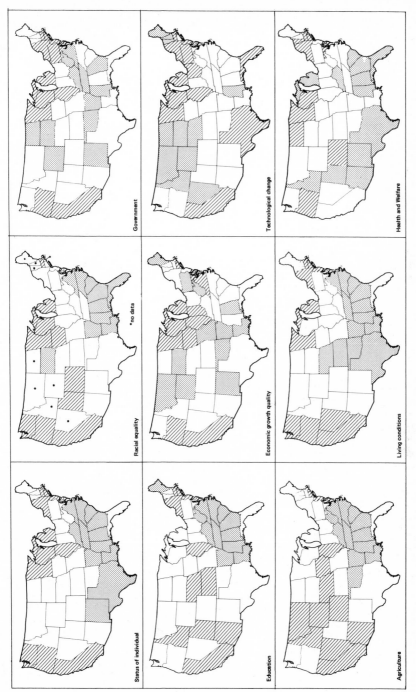

Figure 2.3 The top quarter (shaded) and bottom quarter (dotted) of the forty-eight contiguous states, based on rankings on nine domestic goal areas. (Source of data: Wilson, 1969, 13.)

The geographical patterns are summarized in Figure 2.3. In these maps the top and bottom quarters of the forty-eight contiguous states are identified for each goal area. There are marked similarities between the maps, with the South standing out as a poor region on most criteria and the West Coast and Northwest generally showing up very favorably. The main exceptions are in Technological Change, where the bottom states shift to the northern Rockies and Plains, in Economic Growth where there is a similar pattern, in Agriculture where most of the top states are in the Plains and the West, and in Racial Equality where the Northeast has fewer of the top states than in the other maps.

No geography textbook presently available provides as broad a view of the human geography of the United States as is made possible by the research summarized here. Wilson's study provides an excellent model for further work at the regional level. A similar inter-state study based on the concept of social well-being is presented in Chapter 7 of this book.

REFERENCES CITED

Bell, W. H. and Stevenson, D. W. (1964), "An Index of Economic Health for Ontario Counties and Districts," *Ontario Economic Review*, 2, pp. 1-7.

Berry, B. J. L. (1965), "Identification of Declining Regions: An Empirical Study of the Dimensions of Rural Poverty," in R. S. Thoman and W. D. Wood, eds., *Areas of Economic Stress in Canada*, Queen's University Press, Kingston, Ont., pp. 22-66.

Cole, J. P. and King, C. A. M (1968), *Quantitative Geography*, John Wiley, London and New York, pp. 295-304.

_____ and Smith, G. A. (1967), *An Introduction of Factor Analysis with the United States as an Example*, Bulletin of Quantitative Data for Geographers, No. 8, Dept. of Geography, University of Nottingham (mimeo).

Guertin, W. H. and Bailey, J. P. (1970), *Introduction to Modern Factor Analysis*, Edwards Bros. Inc., Ann Arbor, Mich.

Harman, H. H. (1966), *Modern Factor Analysis*, Chicago University Press, Chicago (2nd edition).

Harries, K. D. (1970), "The Geography of American Crime, 1968," *The Journal of Geography*, 70, pp. 204-213.

Harrington, M. (1962), *The Other America: Poverty in the United States*, Macmillan, New York.

King, L. J. (1969), *Statistical Analysis in Geography*, Prentice-Hall, Englewood Cliffs, N.J., pp. 165-193.

Lewis, G. M. (1968), "Levels of Living in the North-eastern United States c. 1960: A New Approach to Regional Geography," *Transactions of the Institute of British Geographers*, 45, pp. 11-37.

Lowry, M. (1970), "Race and Socio Economic Well-being: A Geographical Analysis of the Mississippi Case," *Geographical Review*, 60, pp. 511-528.

Morrill, R. L. (1965), "The Negro Ghetto: Problems and Alternatives," *Geographical Review*, 55, pp. 339-361.
⎯⎯⎯⎯⎯ (1969), "Geographical Aspects of Poverty in The United States," *Proceedings of the Association of American Goegraphers*, 1, pp. 117-121.
⎯⎯⎯⎯⎯ and Wohlenberg, E. H. (1971), *The Geography of Poverty in the United States*, McGraw-Hill, New York.
Munson, B. E. (1968), *Changing Community Dimensions: The Interrelationship of Social and Economic Variables*, College of Administrative Science, The Ohio State University, Columbus, Ohio.
Peet, R. (1971), "Poor, Hungry America," *Professional Geographer*, 23, pp. 99-104.
President's Commission on National Goals (1960), *Goals for Americans*, Prentice-Hall, Englewood Cliffs, N.J.
Rose, H. M. (1970), "The Development of an Urban Subsystem: The Case of the Negro Ghetto," *Annals of the Association of American Geographers*, 60, pp. 1-17.
⎯⎯⎯⎯⎯ (1971), *The Black Ghetto: A Spatial Behavioral Perspective*, McGraw-Hill, New York.
Rummel, R. J. (1967), "Understanding Factor Analysis," *Journal of Conflict Resolution*, 11.
Smith, D. M. (1968), "Identifying the 'Grey' Areas—A Multivariate Approach," *Regional Studies*, 2, pp. 183-193.
⎯⎯⎯⎯⎯ (1971), "Radical Geography: The Next Revolution?," *Area*, Institute of British Geographers, 3, pp. 153-157.
Thompson, J. H. (1964), "What About a Geography of Poverty?," *Economic Geography*, 40, p. 183.
⎯⎯⎯⎯⎯ et al. (1962), "Towards a Geography of Economic Health," *Annals of the Association of American Geographers*, 52, pp. 1-20.
U.S. Department of Commerce, National Bureau of Standards (1969), *Community Profile: Hillsborough County, Florida*, Office of Economic Opportunity Information Center, Washington, D.C.
Wilson, J. O. (1969), *Quality of Life in the United States: An Excursion into the New Frontier of Socio-Economic Indicators*, Midwest Research Institute, Kansas City, Mo.

CHAPTER 3

THE CLASSIFICATION OF CITIES

The classification of cities has attracted considerable attention from both geographers and sociologists. However, the literature in this field reflects the same bias towards economic variables as is evident in much contemporary regional analysis. In urban geography the "functional classification" approach to the search for a typology of cities in the United States and elsewhere has such a strong tradition that it is only very recently that geographers have been able to break out of this mould.

The Economic Function Approach

Two established classifications of American cities have been particularly influential in studies of urban geography in the United States. The first was by Harris (1943), who used employment and occupational data to classify about 600 urban areas on the basis of their dominant economic function. The second was by Nelson (1955), who also used employment data; he developed a multiple-function economic classification for almost 900 cities, attempting to allocate his cities to classes in a less arbitrary manner than Harris. Their techniques and results are faithfully reproduced in most textbooks, including many of the most recent ones published (for example, see Yeates and Garner, 1971, 63-79). Another well-known economic functional classification is the one which has appeared in the *Municipal Year Book* for more than twenty years.

The economic-function approach to city classification in the United States and elsewhere has been criticized on a number of grounds (see, for example, Smith, 1965). Features subject to such criticism include the arbitrary nature of the way in which cities are allocated to their respective classes, the fact that the categories are not generally mutually exclusive, and the lack of sophistication in the manipulation of the numerical data. Of more fundamental importance is the criticism that the classification is in practically every case an end in itself rather than a point of departure for further research. As Hadden and Borgatta (1965, 70) put it: "a classification system should describe the principal dimensions of a domain of intellectual concern. In other words, attempts at classification suggest to us what the relevant or significant variables of a domain are and thus may be viewed as necessary prerequisites for the development of systematic empirical theory." It would be difficult to argue that economic functional classifications of cities have made any real contribution to empirically based urban theory for the simple reason that they were not undertaken with this in mind.

From the point of view of the present book, the main shortcoming of the functional classification approach, and indeed of much work in urban geography, is its lack of concern for social problem conditions. No social variables of any kind appear in most of these classifications and, as Hadden and Borgatta (1965, 67) stated, it has not been shown empirically that economic specialization is significantly related to other important characteristics of the social milieu. For city classifications based on social criteria it is necessary to look beyond the traditional functional approach, to the work of certain sociologists and contemporary geographers.

Sociological Approaches

As in the case of establishing regional systems, it was the application of factor analysis that first enabled students of urban affairs to classify cities on the basis of a large number of different conditions. The earliest example is in a paper by Price (1942). He took the ninety-three American cities with populations of over 100,000 in 1930, and factor analyzed data on fifteen demographic and socio-economic characteristics. His variables measure social well-being only insofar as they reflect the economic status of the population. The first factor extracted from these data is associated with large cities with low population increases, high rentals, and high wholesale and retail trade. The highest scores on this factor go to the major older cities such as New York, Chicago, Washington, Boston, and San Francisco. The second factor is most closely associated with occupational structure. Hadden and Borgatta (1965, 21) subsequently identified these factors as Population Size and Socio-Economic Status Level.

Price was concerned with identifying the fundamental socio-economic dimensions along which metropolitan centers are differentiated. At about the same time, Angell (1941-42; 1947) attempted to compare cities with respect to a much more specific and restricted concept—that of *social integration*. Angell's first paper is of special interest in the present context, because he chose to use community welfare effort as an indicator of social integration, on the proposition that there would be a "more vital moral order" in communities that shoulder a larger proportion of their local welfare responsibilities. From information on the services provided in twenty-eight major cities, he derived a "Welfare Effort Index" for each place (Angell, 1941-42, 376-377). Very considerable inter-city variations were found (Table 3.1). He then compared these results with a "Crime Index" based on FBI data, but the correlation with the welfare index was

Table 3.1. Classification of twenty-eight cities according to welfare effort and crime

	Welfare Effort Index	Crime Index	Welfare Effort Rank	Crime Rank (reversed)	Mean Rank
"Consistent" Cities					
Well Integrated					
Buffalo	266.7	9.14	1	2	1.5
Milwaukee	199.5	6.22	4	1	2.5
Syracuse	235.6	11.99	2	4	3.0
Springfield (Mass.)	233.5	14.79	3	6	4.5
Providence	148.2	10.20	8	3	5.5
Moderately Integrated					
Baltimore	166.1	24.43	6	12	9.0
Hartford	139.0	27.18	9	14	11.5
Bridgeport	101.4	17.35	16	8	12.0
Cleveland	131.2	33.79	11	17	14.0
St. Louis	89.9	19.46	18	10	14.0
Canton	105.0	32.91	14	16	15.0
San Francisco	101.7	29.81	15	15	15.0
Dayton	93.2	26.15	17	13	15.0
Los Angeles	115.5	43.86	12	21	16.5
Kansas City (Mo.)	83.3	35.32	19	18	18.5
Poorly Integrated					
Houston	63.5	41.89	24.5	19	21.75
Columbus (Ohio)	72.2	55.54	20	26	23.0
Dallas	50.7	45.86	27	22	24.5
Birmingham	62.8	48.54	26	24	25.0
Atlanta	63.5	77.46	24.5	28	26.25
"Inconsistent" Cities					
Crime Index shows more integration than Welfare Effort Index					
New Orleans	71.7	15.07	21	7	14.0
Wichita	65.2	19.34	23	9	16.0
Grand Rapids	65.7	21.73	22	11	16.5
Wilkes-Barre	50.6	14.18	28	5	16.5
Welfare Effort Index shows more integration than Crime Index					
Cincinnati	191.5	42.23	5	20	12.5
Richmond (Va.)	153.6	54.25	7	25	16.0
Indianapolis	132.0	47.90	10	23	16.5
Louisville	111.6	59.83	13	27	20.0

Note: The Welfare Effort Index for a given area (city) is per capita local expenditure (adjusted for level-of-living), multiplied by a fraction whose numerator was the average of the percentages of expenditures that derive from nonlocal sources for all areas and whose denominator was the percentage of expenditures deriving from nonlocal soucres for the particular area. The Crime Index was derived from data on the incidence of murder and non-negligent homicide, robbery, and burglary, with each crime weighted proportional to the square of its frequency.
Source: Angell (1941-2).

not very high $(r = -.393)$. Comparisons were made between the performance of individual cities on the two indices, and Angell was able to classify his cities into "well integrated," "moderately integrated," and "poorly integrated," with the additional category of "inconsistent" cities where the welfare and crime indices were clearly out of line. Members of these classes were compared with respect to other social variables, such as the rates of homicide, suicide, illegitimacy and venereal disease, and these were found to increase significantly with poorer social integration.

On the basis of this first study, Angell determined that the crime index, taken negatively, was the best single indicator of social integration. In his second paper (1947) he took a larger number of cities, and attempted to account for differences in integration. He combined crime with a measure of welfare effort to arrive at an "Integration Index" and this was compared with population mobility, population composition, and other possible independent variables. The multiple correlation between indices of mobility and of composition on the one hand and the integration index on the other was $-.79$. Poor social integration was thus found to be closely associated with high population mobility and with high proportions of certain groups (foreign-born and non-whites) in the city population.

Despite Price's first demonstration, and a paper by Hofstaetter (1952) using the same technique (see below), it was the 1960s before factor analysis became more than an isolated innovation in city classification. The first really large-scale study was that of Moser and Scott (1961) in Britain. A total of 157 towns were included, and there were sixty variables measuring population size and structure, population change, household characteristics and housing, economic character, social class, voting, health and education. Most of the data were from the 1951 Census. Moser and Scott used principal components analysis, and their leading components are: I - Social Class, II - Population Growth, III - Recent Development, and IV - Housing Conditions. This study set the pattern for a number of other attempts at city classification, by both sociologists and geographers.

The Hadden and Borgatta Study of American Cities

The best-known factor analytical study of American cities is that of Hadden and Borgatta (1965). They measured the roughly 650 cities with populations over 25,000, on sixty-five variables concerned with demographic characteristics, income, education, housing, employment, economic activity, location, and age of the city. The data were from the 1960 Census and the *City and County Data Book* and predominantly represent the conventional kind of population and economic statistics usually found in such sources. Their leading factors are: I - Socio-Economic Status Level, II - Nonwhite Population, and III - Age Composition. Scores on these and subsequent factors were used to derive "profiles" for each city, that could be compared one with another and used as a basis for classification. Hadden and Borgatta were very critical of the economic function approach to city classification. They deliberately included variables which would produce some factors representing types of economic specialization, and found that very little of the variance of the other conditions included in the study accrued to these specialization factors (Hadden and Borgatta, 1965, 67).

The basic objective of Hadden and Borgatta was to find the underlying variables in city differentiation, and hence contribute to the development of empirical urban theory. Their context is that of broad socio-economic structure, and they were not concerned with social problems as such. However, scores on their leading factor, which loads high on income, housing, and educational variables (Table 3.2), were interpreted as a "Deprivation Index," and provide a possible indicator of socio-economic well-being.

Table 3.2. Loadings on Hadden and Borgatta's factor 1: Socio-economic Status

Variable	Loading
Percent families $10,000 income and over	.95
Median income of families	.90
Median value owner occupied housing unit	.86
Median gross monthly rent of renter occupied units	.86
Percent employed in white-collar occupations	.78
Percent housing units sound, with all plumbing facilities	.72
Percent college graduates in population 25 years and over	.70
Median school years completed in population 25 years and over	.67
Percent families under $3,000 income	−.65
Percent labor force unemployed	−.62
Persons employed in finance, insurance and real estate per capita	.58
Percent housing units with two or more automobiles	.58
Percent completed less than 5 years school, 25 years and over	−.53

Note: Variables with loadings of less than .50 are not listed. The factor loadings are the weights used in the city Deprivation Index.

Source: Hadden and Borgatta (1965, 41).

Hadden and Borgatta were not greatly concerned with geographical variations in city characteristics. They do say that there are characteristics that "tend to have qualitative aspects associated with regions," for example, the foreign-born association with the Northeast and the Negro association with the South. But they say that it would be foolhardy to imply that these differences are not subject to radical change in time, suggesting their transitory nature: "They may be important to note historically, but there is serious question as to whether such facts can underlie basic urban theory" (Hadden and Borgatta, 1965, 71).

Observations of the association of particular classes of cities with particular parts of the country are of interest to the geographer in a purely descriptive sense, if in no other way. Scores on the Deprivation Index have been mapped (leaving out cities of less than 50,000 people for clarity), with a separate map for each quintile (Figure 3.1). Some important differences in the five patterns can be observed. Cities in the *top quintile* (the "best" fifth of the cities, or the least deprived) have their biggest concentration in the Los Angeles area, with others in suburbs of major cities such as Detroit and Cleveland. There is also a significant scatter in the Plains, centered on Iowa. The *second quintile* shows a similar general pattern, comprising a discontinuous and fairly narrow belt from Lake Erie to California, with additions in New England. The main concentrations are still on the West Coast and in the Midwest. The *third quintile* shows less of a scatter across the nation. The emphasis has shifted to the New York and New Jersey suburbs, and a small group has appeared in Texas and

Figure 3.1 The performance of American cities on Hadden and Borgatta's Deprivation Index. The lines on maps (a) to (e) are "median axes" with an origin in Boston, dividing the pattern of dots into two equal parts. Note that the quintile maps include only cities of 50,000 population or more, while the state average map includes all cities with populations of 25,000 or more. (Source of data: Hadden and Borgatta, 1965, 76-100.)

Oklahoma. The Midwest concentration has retracted to the area east of the Mississippi, and there are less than before on the West Coast. The *fourth quintile* includes many of the industrial cities of the major manufacturing belt in Ohio, Pennsylvania and New York, and also cities in the lower Mississippi basin. There are now very few in the West. The *bottom quintile*, comprising the "worst" fifth of the cities, is very different from the other patterns, with almost all the cities south and east of a line from Boston to El Paso. The main concentration is in the "old South," with extensions into the north representing the poorer cities of the manufacturing belt, especially in Pennsylvania and New Jersey.

It is clear from the maps that deprivation in cities is subject to a quite regular areal variation. A "median axis" drawn through the dots on each map so as to divide them in half, with an origin placed (arbitrarily) on Boston, shifts steadily south after being in roughly the same position for the first two quintiles (north of Los Angeles), to cut through Phoenix, Arizona, for the third quintile, south of El Paso, Texas, for the fourth quintile, and through New Orleans for the bottom quintile. Thus, after the top two categories, deprivation gets steadily greater towards the southeastern corner of the USA.

Another way to show how deprivation varies within the United States is to calculate state averages from individual city scores. A "State Weighted City Deprivation Index" (S) has been calculated as follows:

$$S = \frac{\sum\limits_{i=1}^{n} I_i \times P_i}{\sum\limits_{i=1}^{n} P_i}$$

where I_i = Index of Deprivation (i.e., decile score) for city i
P_i = population of city i
n = number of cities with populations of 25,000 or more in the state.

In other words, for each state in turn the population of each city is multiplied by its Deprivation Index, the results are added, and the sum is divided by the sum of the city populations. This gives a state index which can vary from 0 to 9, like the decile scores. Deprivation increases with the size of the index. The map of these scores (Figure 3.1f) shows the extent to which the average state level of city deprivation varies in a regular manner across the nation. Based on data for all cities with 25,000 inhabitants or more, the map accounts for about 45 percent of the American population.

The Contemporary Geographical Approach

Since geographers began to use factor analysis, their work on city classification has closely resembled that of Moser and Scott (1961) and Hadden and Borgatta (1965). Two of the best-known geographical studies are those of Ahmad (1965) on Indian cities and King (1966) on Canadian cities. In both cases, over fifty variables are used, and they are almost entirely concerned with demographic and economic conditions. Of Ahmad's sixty-two variables, only three relate to households and housing, four to health, and two to social amenities. King's variables have even less strictly social content.

The latest and greatest of these multivariate analyses is the new social and economic grouping of American cities prepared for the 1970 edition of the *Municipal Year Book* (Forstall, 1970), based on a massive statistical analysis directed by Brian Berry. This replaces the old economic function-al city classification reproduced for years in this book—a rather significant sign of the times and of the increasing concern for social as against economic conditions, even if this new classification does not really include much information on social problems. The task of compiling data on 1761 cities ensured that only readily-available published sources would be used and it is not surprising that the ninty-seven variables closely resemble those used in previous socio-economic classifications. One further out-come of this study is a useful methodological handbook (Berry, 1972), which provides an up-to-date summary of the present state of city classification in geography.

Deficiencies in Current Approaches

From the point of view of the present research focus on social well-being, the contemporary work of both geographers and sociologists is unsatisfac-tory in a number of respects. The most serious are their empiricism and their selection of variables. There has generally been an assiduous avoiding of a priori theorizing or conceptualization; as King (1966) remarked of Moser and Scott (1961) and Ahmad (1965), "The studies of British towns and Indian cities were exploratory in the sense that they were not structured around any hypothesis or the testing of any theory. In fact, these studies appear conspicuously devoid of any reference to theory." In some cases this was quite intentional; Hadden and Borgatta (1965, 18) say, "Rather than imposing *ad hoc* conceptualizations on the data, we wanted to explore the possibility of deriving some independent underlying dimensions on which cities should be characterized and differentiated." The problem is that what comes out is partially determined by what goes in when factor or components analysis is used. And what goes in is dependent on the data available, as Moser and Scott (1961, 76) readily admitted.

So the discussion returns to the question of the adequacy of existing data. In reality, the numerical input to the kind of city analyses described above is determined by the conditions that the Census Bureau and other governmental data collection agencies decide should be measured, and by what other information is published in a convenient form for use in research. If some conditions are overlooked, judged to be unimportant, or simply incapable of measurement by existing methods, then they will not be included. As has been pointed out earlier, existing official statistical series are heavily biased towards measuring economic conditions, and social conditions of great importance are sometimes ignored.

A form of a priori conceptualization has thus already taken place, imposing limits to the choice of variables that Hadden and Borgatta and the others were likely to use. It can hardly be claimed that underlying dimensions of city differentiation can be obtained by factor analyzing the content of the census when what the census measures may be based on an outdated paradigm that gives undue emphasis to certain aspects of national life. The general omission from existing city classifications of data on a wide range of social pathologies is a consequence of this initial selectivity brought to bear on the nature of the numerical input. Insofar as these neglected conditions are a significant part of the nature of cities, empirically derived theory based on the results of these studies will be incomplete.

The "Goodness" of Cities

To find a study of American cities that gives adequate treatment to conditions such as social pathologies, it is necessary to go back to the end of the 1930s. It was then that a remarkable book was published by Thorndike (1939; see also Thorndike and Woodyard, 1937, and Thorndike, 1940), a work that is, in effect, an attempt to describe and explain differences between cities in the quality of life. This book has been entirely overlooked by urban geographers and, as Hadden and Borgatta (1965, 22) point out, in the literature on city classification in general.

Thorndike's main study (1939) was based on an analysis of the 310 cities with populations of over 30,000 in 1930. About 300 variables were considered initially, and these were then narrowed down to thirty-seven all or nearly all of which "reasonable persons will regard as significant for the goodness of life for good people" (Thorndike, 1939, 22). These fall under the headings of health, education, recreation, economic and social conditions, creature comforts, and "other items." The list of variables is quite different from that usually found in subsequent socio-economic city classifications, and includes, among other things, morbidity rates for selected illnesses (including venereal diseases), per capita public park acreage, expenditures on libraries and museums, and the circulation of certain literary material (see Table 3.3 for full list).

Thorndike proceeded to weight each of the thirty-seven variables by what appears to be a combination of statistical analysis and subjective judgement. Then for each city a composite index or "G-score" was obtained. The correlation between these scores and various possible independent variables was established. The best predictors were found to be the personal qualities of the population (based on an index of a number of different characteristics), and private income. Thorndike (1939, 67) interpreted his general findings as follows:

> Cities are made better than others in this country primarily and chiefly by getting able and good people as residents. . . . The second i rtant cause of welfare is income. Good people, rich or poor, earning much or earning little, are a good thing for a city, but the more they have and earn the better. They and their incomes account for at least three-fourths, and probably more, of the differences of American cities in the goodness of life for good people.

G-scores were found to correlate significantly in a negative direction with blacks as a proportion of total population ($r = -.60$), a reflection of the effects of a long history of racial discrimination. A particularly interesting

Table 3.3. Constituents of Thorndike's G-score

Item	Approximate Weight
Items of Health	
Infant death-rate (reversed)	12
General death-rate (reversed)	9½
Typhoid death-rate (reversed)	5
Appendicitis death-rate (reversed)	4
Puerperal diseases death-rate (reversed)	4
Items of Education	
Per capita public expenditures for schools	8
Per capita public expenditures for teachers' salaries	6
Per capita public expenditures for textbooks and supplies	7
Per capita public expenditures for libraries and museums	6½
Percentage of persons sixteen to seventeen attending schools	4½
Percentage of persons eighteen to twenty attending schools	7
Average salary high school teacher	4½
Average salary elementary school teacher	3½
Items of Recreation	
Per capita public expenditures for recreation	7
Per capita acreage of public parks	2½
Economic and "Social" Items	
Rarity of extreme poverty	6
Rarity of less extreme poverty	6
Infrequency of gainful employment for boys 10-14	5
Infrequency of gainful employment for girls 10-14	5½
Average wage of workers in factories	4
Frequency of home ownership (per capita number of homes owned)	6
Per capita support of the Y.M.C.A.	6
Excess of physicians, nurses, and teachers over male domestic servants	6
Creature Comforts	
Per capita domestic installations of electricity	5
Per capita domestic installation of gas	7
Per capita number of automobiles	4
Per capita domestic installations of telephones	11
Per capita domestic installation of radios	6½
Other Items	
Percent of literacy in the total population	3½
Per capita circulation of *Better Homes and Gardens, Good Housekeeping* and the *National Geographic Magazine*	6
Per capita circulation of the *Literary Digest*	6
Death rate from syphilis (reversed)	4
Death rate from homicide (reversed)	3½
Death rate from automobile accidents (reversed)	4½
Per capita value of asylums, schools, libraries, museums, and parks owned by the public	6
Ratio of value of schools, etc., to value of jails, etc.	10
Per capita public property minus public debt	5

Source: Thorndike (1939, 189-191).

finding was the weak negative correlation between G and church membership per capita ($r = -.22$); high church membership appeared to be affiliated with typical features of traditional morality like low rates of homicide, venereal disease and illegitimacy, rather than with low levels of poverty and other forms of social deprivation (Thorndike, 1939, 49).

Thorndike was interested in what he described as "errors in opinions" about cities. He computed an index of 117 cities based on twenty-three variables "which would be regarded by all competent persons as indicative of the goodness of life for good people," taken from the original thirty-seven variables. He then compared these indices with ratings derived from local leaders in education, religion, philanthropy and business. The opinions of these individuals were found to give too little weight to health, education, poverty, and creature comforts, i.e., Thorndike's index correlates highly with these conditions. The leaders were found to give too much stress to park acreages, value of property, and size of a city, i.e., the composite score based on their ratings correlates well with these phenomena but poorly with infant mortality reversed, general death rate reversed, education variables, and per capita availability of certain things indicative of good material living standards. In other words, the leaders were found to judge cities too much by the conspicuous things which their social equals could be expected to value (i.e., they reflected elite attitudes), while they were less concerned with the conditions of the population at large.

Perhaps the best example of the inaccurate perception of the goodness of life in cities is to be found with the southern cities (Thorndike, 1939, 145-146). "Southern cities for the richer quarter of the native-born white

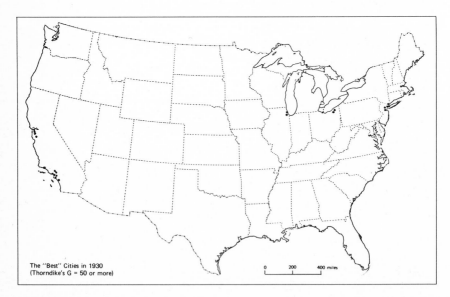

The "Best" Cities in 1930
(Thorndike's G = 50 or more)

0   200   400 miles

Figure 3.2 The "best" cities in 1930, on a goodness of life score. (Source of data: Thorndike, 1939, 33-34.)

population, may be, or at least seems to these educators, clergymen, and businessmen to be, well up to the average for American cities. But these cities were notable for infant mortality, homicides, syphilis, illiteracy, extreme poverty, child labor, low wages, lack of libraries, and lack of creature comforts for large sections of the population." The inability or

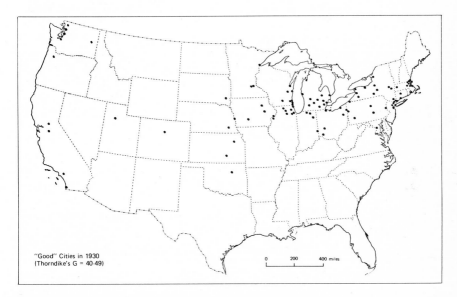

"Good" Cities in 1930
(Thorndike's G = 40-49)

0   200   400 miles

Figure 3.3 The "good" cities in 1930, on a goodness of life score. (Source of data: Thorndike, 1939, 33-34.)

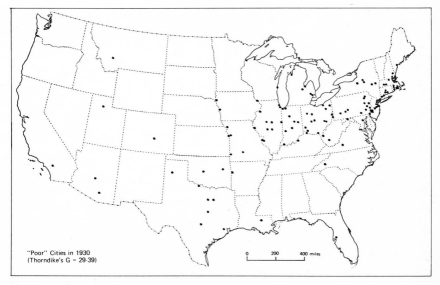

"Poor" Cities in 1930
(Thorndike's G = 29-39)

0   200   400 miles

Figure 3.4 The "poor" cities in 1930, on a goodness of life score. (Source of data: Thorndike, 1939, 33-34.)

unwillingness of national and community leaders to perceive accurately the conditions of life for the majority in these cities, and in cities elsewhere in the United States, may have a great deal to do with the persistence of a low quality of life up to the present time.

Thorndike was not really concerned with geographical aspects of the goodness of cities, but there is much of geographical interest in his results. An analysis of the G-scores for cities of over 30,000 population shows systematic areal variations, and a tendency for good and bad cities to concentrate in certain regions of the country. To illustrate this, the cities have been divided into four classes on the basis of their G-scores. This has been done with the aid of a frequency distribution, which suggests some

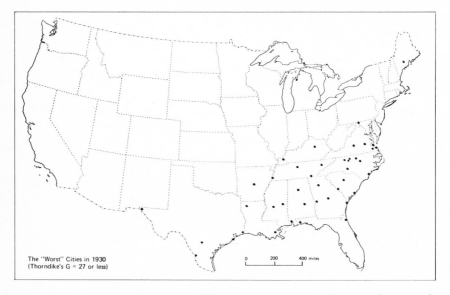

The "Worst" Cities in 1930
(Thorndike's G = 27 or less)

0   200   400 miles

Figure 3.5 The "worst" cities in 1930, on a goodness of life score. (Source of data: Thorndike, 1939, 33-34.)

fairly obvious class limits. Members of each class have been mapped (Figures 3.2, 3.3, 3.4, and 3.5), and the following brief comments describe the nature of the location patterns observed:

The "Best Cities" (G = 50 or more). These are very highly concentrated in the Los Angeles and San Francisco suburbs in the West and in the New York-New Jersey suburbs in the East. The only places not suburbs are the resort of Colorado Springs, and San Jose and Santa Barbara.

The "Good" Cities (G = 40-49). The highest scores in this class (46 or more) still occur frequently in the Boston and New Jersey suburbs, but there are quite a number in the upper Midwest, especially Michigan. There are none south of a line from Staten Island to San Diego. As the 40-45 scores are plotted the major manufacturing belt takes on a clear form, with something of an extension into the farming areas of the Plains. On the West Coast, Washington has more "good" cities than California. There is nothing in this whole class below a line from Washington, D.C., to San Diego via Tulsa.

The "Poor" Cities (G = 29-39). Cities in the top half of this class (G = 35 or more) tend to be in the southern half of the major manufacturing belt, i.e., in Illinois, Indiana, Ohio, and Pennsylvania. Few are outside this area. As the G-scores drop under 35 there is some spread into Oklahoma and Texas, but south of the northern Tennessee and North Carolina border and east of the Mississippi River only Baton Rouge, Tampa, and Asheville appear.

The "Worst" Cities (G = 27 or less). These cities are heavily concentrated in the South, a fact which is at least partly attributed to the low quality of life for blacks, who in 1930 were still very much confined to this part of the country. Lewiston in Maine is an isolated exception. All cities in this class are south and east of a line from New York to El Paso. The "worst" cities thus fill the gap conspicuously empty in the previous maps when the eastern half of the country is examined.

This pattern of areal differentiation agrees quite closely with that indicated by Hadden and Borgatta's Deprivation Index (Figure 3.1), although Thorndike's variables were not the same and his method of scoring was less sophisticated. Thorndike's work was a few years too early to take advantage of factor analysis, of course. However, Hofstaetter (1952) later took Thorndike's data on twenty-three of the thirty-seven variables, intercorrelated them, and performed a factor analysis. His leading factors are: I - Prevalence of Slum Conditions, II - Enlightened Affluence, III - Industrialization, and IV - Organized Public Welfare. The structure revealed thus departs considerably from that found by Hadden and Borgatta.

Thorndike's book provides the nearest thing there is to a model approach to the study of social well-being at the inter-city level. His G-score can be regarded as the first set of urban indicators with the capacity to reflect a wide range of criteria of the quality of life. If this study was possible in the 1930s it would be no less feasible today and an updated version could provide a far better set of urban social indicators than anything currently available. Chapter 8 describes some attempts at inter-city analyses from a contemporary social indicators perspective.

REFERENCES CITED

Ahmad, Q. (1965), *Indian Cities: Characteristics and Correlates*, Research Paper No. 102, Dept. of Geography, University of Chicago.

Angell, R. C. (1941-42), "The Social Integration of Selected American Cities," *American Journal of Sociology*, 47, pp. 575-592.

_____ (1947), "The Social Integration of American Cities of More Than 100,000 Population," *American Sociological Review*, 12, pp. 335-342.

Berry, B. J. L., ed. (1972), *City Classification Handbook: Methods and Applications*, John Wiley, New York.

Forstall, R. L. (1970), "A New Social and Economic Grouping of Cities," in *The Municipal Year Book 1970*, The International City Management Association, Washington, D.C., pp. 102-159.

Hadden, J. K. and Borgatta, E. F. (1965), *American Cities: Their Social Characteristics*, Rand McNally, Chicago.

Harris, C. D. (1943), "A Functional Classification of Cities in the United States," *Geographical Review*, 33, pp. 86-99.

Hofstaetter, P. R. (1952), "Your City—Revisited: A Factorial Study of Cultural Patterns," *American Catholic Sociological Review*, 13, pp. 159-168.

King, L. J. (1966), "Cross-Sectional Analysis of Canadian Urban Dimensions: 1951 and 1961," *Canadian Geographer*, 10, pp. 205-224.

Moser, C. A. and Scott, W. (1961), *British Towns: A Statistical Study of their Social and Economic Differences*, Oliver and Boyd, Edinburgh and London.

Nelson, H. J. (1955), "A Service Classification of American Cities," *Economic Geography*, 31, pp. 189-201.

Price, D. O. (1942), "Factor Analysis in the Study of Metropolitan Centers," *Social Forces*, 20, pp. 449-455.

Smith, R. H. T. (1965), "Method and Purpose in Functional Town Classification," *Annals of the Association of American Geographers*, 55, pp. 539-548.

Thorndike, E. L. (1939), *Your City*, Harcourt, Brace and Co., New York.

_____ (1940), *144 Smaller Cities*, Harcourt, Brace and Co., New York.

_____ and Woodyard, E. (1937), "Individual Differences in American Cities: Their Nature and Causation," *American Journal of Sociology*, 43, pp. 191-224.

Yeates, M. H. and Garner, B. J. (1971), *The City in America*, Harper and Row, New York, pp. 60-87.

CHAPTER 4

URBAN
SOCIAL
GEOGRAPHY

Of the three spatial levels of analysis under review here—the inter-state, inter-city, and intra-city—it is at the latter level that most work has been done on the spatial incidence of social problems. This can be attributed largely to the start given to this kind of ecological analysis by the "Chicago School" of urban sociology.

The Chicago School of Urban Sociology

Almost half a century ago, Park, Burgess and McKenzie (1925) put forward their concentric zone model of urban spatial structure. In it, cities were arranged in a series of concentric zones, with the predominant land use changing from commercial through industrial and increasingly high qualities of residential development, from the city center to the periphery. People were seen as moving successively outwards from the inner city where immigrants were first assimilated, into better residential areas, as their social mobility increased with improved economic ,status. This dynamic view of the social geography of cities was influenced by work in plant ecology, and embodied the idea of the invasion of a "natural area" of one group by a competing group leading to "succession" and to the dominance of the area by the new group.

Although this model was too rigid to have wide generality, it did provide a framework within which more detailed empirical research could be conducted on urban social patterns. Major studies of various aspects of social disorganization were produced by the Chicago School, the best known including Faris and Dunham (1939) on mental disorders and Shaw and McKay (1942) on juvenile delinquency. The approach has been summarized by Michelson (1970, 8-9) as follows:

> They typically studied a phenomenon (usually a pathology such as crime or mental illness) at an aggregate level, having divided the city into a number of

39

subareas corresponding as much as possible to natural areas. They explained the
existence of the phenomenon by referring to the homogeneous social organization to be found within the subarea, which in turn was dependent on the spatial
relations of that place to surrounding subareas. Since the people or use of an
area often changed, the character of a natural area at any point in time would be
a function of the constant competition for space and hierarchy of dominance;
therefore the pathologies usually found their explanation in an unalterable cause
with strong economic overtones.

The concentric zone model was in fact an expression of the way
competition for space within a city is played out in the urban land
market. Particular uses or groups occupy an area by virtue of their
rent-paying capacity.

The research method in these ecological studies relied on the identification of natural community areas for which aggregate numerical data could
be compiled. Areas of the city, defined as groups of census tracts, would
be given scores or indices with respect to a particular condition. These
scores, when mapped and compared with the patterns of incidence of
other conditions, made possible the search for relationships among
variables. Scores might be added up by concentric zones, and the
regularity of change with distance from the city center observed.

The study of delinquency by Shaw and McKay (1942) exemplifies the
work of these urban ecologists. They found the distribution of delinquency to be highly correlated with the physical and social organizational
characteristics of the city. Rates declined on a regular gradient with
distance from the center of Chicago, as revealed by data for concentric
distance bands. This zonal pattern prevailed also for rates of truancy,
infant mortality, tuberculosis, and mental disorder. Delinquency and these
other pathologies were found to be highly correlated with substandard
housing and other physical signs of neighborhood deterioration, family
dependence on relief and so on, little home ownership, and certain other
social and economic conditions. Shaw and McKay argued that the
common causative factor in the distribution of delinquency and other
social pathologies is social disorganization, or the breakdown and inadequacy of previously functioning institutions and social arrangements.

Subsequently, both the theory and the methodology of classical social
ecology has been questioned (see for example Theodorson, 1961;
Schnore, 1965; Michelson, 1970). The biological analogy has been
queried, as has the concept of social disorganization as the basic cause of
urban social problems. And there are considerable technical difficulties (as
well as theoretical ones) associated with the making of ecological correlations and inferring individual conditions from aggregate data. Nevertheless, the general interest in the spatial incidence of social problems
demonstrated by the Chicago School provides an important basis for
contemporary urban social analysis, and is highly relevant to the geography of social well-being at the intra-city level.

Social Area Analysis and Factorial Ecology

A second approach to the spatial social structure of urban areas that has
been of great influence is social area analysis, as developed by Shevky,

Bell, and Williams (Shevky and Williams, 1949; Bell, 1952; Shevky and Bell, 1955). From a number of postulates concerning the nature of industrial society they derived three basic constructs or characteristics of modern society, relating to the way in which urban populations are differentiated. These were called Social Rank by Shevky (and Economic Status by Bell), Urbanization (Family Status) and Segregation (Ethnic Status). They then proposed three indices to measure these constructs, with data derived from census variables. Scores on these indices were used to classify census tracts into social areas. In some research these indices are used as independent variables in hypotheses, with aspects of social organization as the dependent variable.

Social area analysis has been criticized, on the grounds that the constructs should not have been arrived at in an a priori fashion, but should have been empirically determined by the patterns assumed by the variables (see for example Hawley and Duncan, 1957; Murdie, 1969, 19-25). This is similar to the argument raised over city classification concerning the avoidance of prior conceptualization in the choice of input data. The logical extension of this argument, as expressed by Rees (1970, 316), is that "many more variables detailing the socio-economic characteristics of census tract populations should be included in the study, and that factor analysis should be used to isolate the fundamental patterns of variation in the data, be they Shevky's and Bell's constructs and patterns or nay."

This is the basic proposition behind what is now usually termed the "factorial ecology" approach to urban social geography. Factor analysis was already available at the time of the initial work on social area analysis, and Bell (1955) answered some critics by using this technique on the census data for Los Angeles and San Francisco to reveal a structure consistent with the original Shevky formulation. Subsequently, a number of other major factor analytical studies of single cities have been published, among the most important ones being Rees (1970) on Chicago, Murdie (1969) on Toronto, and Robson (1969) on Sunderland in England. Studies of American cities have, by and large, succeeded in isolating the three general factors of socio-economic status, family status and ethnic status proposed by Shevky, from data on a wide range of social, demographic and economic conditions. Currently there is much interest in comparative factorial ecology (Berry, 1971; Rees, 1972) as attempts are made to see what common spatial structural characteristics there may be in cities in different parts of the world.

As an illustration of factorial ecology research, the study of Chicago by Rees (1970) may be described briefly. He compiled data in fifty-seven socio-economic and demographic variables, for 222 subdivisions of the Chicago SMSA, and performed a factor analysis. The first factor, accounting for 17.8 percent of the total variance, clearly represented Socio-economic Status, with high loadings on occupation, education, and income variables. The second factor (14.2% of variance) could be identified as Stage in the Life Cycle, with high loadings on family size, age variables, and certain housing conditions. The third factor was termed

Race and Resources (13.1% of variance), loading high on blacks as a proportion of total population, low-status employment, low incomes, and poor housing. Subsequent factors, in order of percentage explained variance, were Immigrant and Catholic Status (10.8%), Population Size and Density (7.5%), Jewish and Russian Population (3.8%), Housing Built in 1940s - Workers Commute by Car (3.0%), Irish and Swedish Population (2.6%), Mobility (2.4%), and Other Non-white Population and Italians (2.1%). These ten leading factors accounted for 77.3 percent of the variance in the original fifty-seven variables.

Areal factor scores were then mapped, to reveal the geographical patterns of performance on specific social dimensions. The scores can also be used for multivariate areal classification. As an illustration, Rees plotted scores on Factor 1, Socio-economic Status, against those on Factor 2, Stage in Life Cycle, to produce four classes of areas (Figure 4.1).

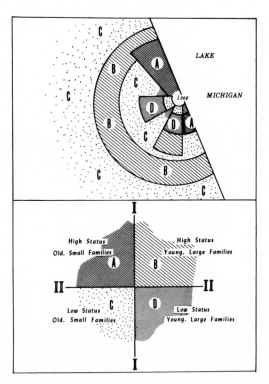

Figure 4.1 Social Areas of the Chicago Metropolis, based on a factorial ecology analysis. (Source: Rees, 1970, 379; Copyright Prentice-Hall Inc., reproduced by permission from B. J. L. Berry and F. Horton, eds., *Geographical Perspectives on Urban Systems.*

When membership of these classes is mapped and generalized, an interesting pattern emerges, combining elements of the concentric zone scheme of classical urban social ecology and the sectoral arrangement of residential areas as proposed by Hoyt (1933, 1939). Rees's Chicago study comprises one of the most thorough and penetrating analyses of the social geography of a single city yet to be published, and exemplifies the best of the contemporary work in factorial ecology.

Deficiencies of the Factorial Ecology Approach

In the general approach and in the specific techniques of analysis used, factorial ecology as currently practiced is very similar to the multifactor regionalization and multivariate socio-economic classification of cities outlined in previous chapters. It is thus open to some of the same criticisms. While there is some merit to the argument that a wide variety of conditions should be analyzed initially so that the basic dimensions of variance that emerge will not be predetermined by the selection of the input data, this can easily be a rationalization for the not uncommon approach of throwing the entire census into the computer to see what comes out. Allowing the Census Bureau to determine or constrain the choice of input data might be justified initially, while new techniques of analysis are developed. But in urban geography a more rigorous basis for discrimination in the selection of variables can now be expected.

That the current factorial ecology approach relies very heavily on the content of census reports can be confirmed by looking at the lists of variables included. As Murdie (1969, 32-38) shows in a tabulation of the major variable types and sources used in these studies, the census is the major (often the only) source in the United States and elsewhere. The variables differ little from those used in multivariate city classifications, the main difference being more social variables relating to such matters as ethnic origin, religious affiliation, demographic character such as age structure, and conditions of housing. Employment data are less conspicuous than in the inter-city studies. Thus the choice of variables seems generally to be guided by some notion of what is important to the *social* character of areas, but the conceptual basis for the selection is very seldom specified.

There is one major omission in all these studies, and that is an adequate representation of social pathologies and other conditions related to social problems in its broadest sense. These data are not available in the census reports, and to compile them from original sources on a tract-by-tract basis is a time consuming task (though by no means impossible, as the Chicago social ecologists showed). As at the inter-city level, it cannot be claimed that the factorial ecology approach is identifying basic dimensions of spatial variation when some important conditions of human existence are not included.

The factorial ecology approach offers an obvious way in which to tackle the problem of areal variations in social well-being within cities. It has the capacity to consider many variables simultaneously, and relate them to basic social spatial patterns within cities. It also has the capacity to analyze trends over time, as Brown and Horton (1970) have shown in their factorial study of changes in Chicago between 1951 and 1961, a very important consideration in the context of social indicators, where the question of whether things are getting better or worse arises. As at the inter-city level, what is needed is to combine some of the powerful techniques developed in the factorial ecology approach to sets of data that more accurately and fully reflect social well-being or the quality of life than the contents of the census and other official sources of readily-available data. The concept of social pathology, or illness, when coupled with the usual content of the factorial ecology studies, would come quite close to encompassing the broad range of variables contributing to social well-being.

Geographical Perspectives on Some Urban Social Pathologies

With the early start given it by the Chicago School in the 1920s and 1930s, there is a strong tradition in sociology of studying the spatial incidence of social problems in cities. Such studies are relatively rare in geographical literature, however. In a bibliography on spatial dimensions of social organization, Jakle (1970) lists 131 publications under the heading of human ecology, in a survey largely confined to the post-World War II period. Less than ten are by geographers, or published in geographical periodicals. He lists fifty-four publications under the heading of social area analysis and factorial ecology, and only five come from geography. This is further evidence that geographers have been singularly lax in their attention to social conditions in cities.

The literature surveyed by Jakle indicates the wide range of conditions that have been investigated through a social ecological approach. Reading from the titles of the publications his list reveals the following: alcoholism, homicide, functional psychoses, mental disorders, marriage instability, illegitimacy, racial violence, mortality, juvenile delinquency, physical and mental health, tax delinquency, schizophrenia and manic depression, crime, vice, social deviance, and vandalism. Thus, much work has already been done on the incidence of many of the normally recognized social problems in urban areas, but there is still very great scope for geographical research of a highly "relevant" nature.

The current "urban crisis" in the United States is increasing interest in the incidence of social problems in cities. Of special public concern at present are poverty, crime, drug abuse, and civil disorder. All have attracted spatial research and some illustrations may be presented briefly.

Poverty is generally recognized as being at the root of many of the other social problems of the city. It is also a condition that attracts particular attention in a society that puts a high value on personal income and on the capacity of the individual to provide for the material wants of himself and his dependents without outside assistance. Much work has been done on the definition of poverty areas within American cities, particularly by the U.S. Department of Commerce, Bureau of the Census (1967) and the U.S. Office of Economic Opportunity (1966). The criteria used are a combination of economic and social factors: income, children not living with parents, years of schooling, unskilled males in the employed labor force, and dilapidated housing. The data are as reported for tracts by the 1960 Census, and designation within a poverty area is based on lowest-quartile performance within a national array on these variables, subject to a few contiguity constraints. The purpose of such a classification, according to the U.S. Department of Commerce (1967, 1) is "to identify target areas for antipoverty programs, to describe the characteristics of the poor residing in areas of concentrated poverty, and to provide a bench mark from which to measure changes in the size and composition of the population in urban slums." Similar methods are in use in defining urban renewal target areas. A major question raised by this approach is whether the traditional essentially economic concept of poverty is broad enough to represent the full range of conditions associated with social deprivation, and interest is now shifting towards the incidence of social problems.

Crime is perhaps the most conspicuous of the (supposedly) poverty-related problems of the city, if only because of its regular measurement by the FBI and the publicity that the annual increase attracts. Less attention is given to the other social problems or pathologies that tend to be associated spatially with crime in the modern city. With considerable eloquence and persuasion, Ramsey Clark (1970, 53-57) remarked of the American city that when poor education, poor employment, poor housing, poor health and so on are marked on a map, and then high crime, the same area is identified every time. Precise empirical support for such a statement is at present lacking, and there is clearly considerable scope for research at the intra-city level aimed at finding out how far crime (and many other conditions) is indicative of the general local level of social well-being (Smith, 1972).

The incidence of crime and delinquency in cities appears to have attracted more ecological or geographical research than any other major social problem. Decreases in crime rates with distance from the city center have been observed (Lottier, 1938; Wolfgang, 1968, 273), correlation and factor-analytical studies have been conducted (e.g., Schmid, 1960), and studies seeking to relate the incidence of delinquency to characteristics of the population of sub-areas of cities (Wolfgang, 1968, 276-278) have been added to the classic work of Shaw and McKay (1942). The current public interest in urban crime rates is illustrated by two recent full-page stories in *The New York Times* (Feb. 14 and 15, 1972) concerning crime report and arrest rates as they vary by precinct, and including maps.

At present, few urban social problems are attracting as much public concern as drug abuse. Although the incidence of this condition is very difficult to measure, the more extreme manifestations such as heroin addiction appear to be both highly concentrated spatially and closely related with general social deprivation. Some evidence to this effect is provided by a recent study of the problem in Washington, D.C. (DuPont, 1971). The number of addicts in each of nine broad areas of the city was estimated, and the highest percentage incidence was found in the Model Cities area (Area 6) which begins four blocks from the United States Capitol and six blocks from the White House. Area levels of addiction were found to correspond closely with crime rates and other indicators of poverty and social disorganization. Table 4.1 compares the number of heroin addicts with four other conditions, and rank correlation coefficients show the high degree of spatial association.

That large-scale riots could occur in the American city was demonstrated in the second half of the 1960s, and there is still a danger that this kind of civil disorder could be repeated. These occurrences are an extreme

Table 4.1. The relationship between heroin addiction and other selected social conditions, in Washington, D.C.

Area No.	Estimated Heroin Addicts		Population Density (1000/mile²)		Poor Families (1000s)		Welfare Cases		Juvenile Court Referrals	
	No.	Rank	No.	Rank	No.	Rank	No.	Rank	No.	Rank
1	1109	6	12.8	5	4.0	9	748	6	290	6
2	571	8	7.9	7	1.6	8	421	8	187	7
3	1848	5	13.2	4	5.2	4	1804	5	268	3
4	2083	4	11.7	6	5 0	5	1815	4	558	5
5	2385	3	17.3	3	7.6	3	2289	3	560	4
6	4066	1	30.9	1	12 4	1	3889	1	1051	1
7	4066	1	29.3	2	11.9	2	2923	2	709	2
8	67	9	5.9	9	4 6	7	71	9	51	9
9	605	7	7.6	8	4.8	6	729	7	150	8

Spearman's Rank Correlation Coefficient with Number of Addicts	0.925	0.981	0.991	0.925

Source of data: DuPont (1971, Tables Three and Four).

indication of social sickness, and the areas in which they arise are generally the ghettos where social well-being is at a low level. A study of the social context of the Watts riot in Los Angeles has demonstrated the coincidence of civil disorder and specific social conditions (Lessing, 1968; Abler, Adams, and Gould, 1971, 153-154). On a map of the city were plotted the areas with median incomes of less than $5,000, blacks more than 75 percent of the population, highest population density, high school dropout rate, and high crime rates, and all these conditions were found to coincide in Watts. This is illustrated in Figure 4.2. Empirically, certain social conditions were thus shown to be capable of defining the location of the riot. However, no general claim can be made that specific characteristics of social deprivation and racial injustice are necessary conditions for civil disorder, and they are certainly not sufficient conditions (Banfield, 1968).

These brief illustrations of the spatial incidence of poverty, crime, drug addiction, and civil disorder in American cities emphaisze the prevalence of a univariate view of such problems. Broader studies relating to social well-being are found less frequently. However, there are some that deal with multivariate concepts such as social disorganization, with a range of social problems, or with hypotheses proposing that one condition can predict or be predicted by a number of others. Two studies of Honolulu illustrate this kind of approach. In a classic early ecological investigation, Lind (1930) examined community disorganization through indices of dependency, juvenile delinquency, vice, and suicide, calculated by districts of the city, and developed a Composite Index of Disorganization. More recently, Schmitt (1966) investigated the effect of overcrowding and population density on social pathology in Honolulu by considering death

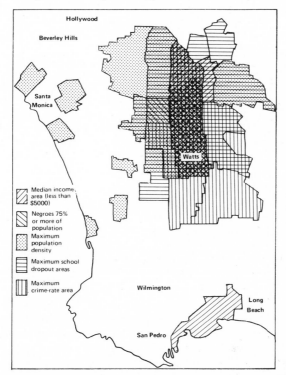

Figure 4.2   The coincidence of various social problem conditions in the area of the Watts riot in Los Angeles. (Source: Lessing, 1968.)

rates, infant mortality, tuberculosis, venereal disease, mental hospitaliza- tion, illegitimacy, juvenile delinquency, and imprisonment. Examples from Europe are the study by Gronholm (1960) of social disorganization in Finland, the work of Castle and Gittus (1957) on social defects in Liverpool, a study of social deviants in Luton by Timms (1965), and a study of social disorganization in Barry in South Wales by Giggs (1970).

The McHarg Approach

A multivariate approach to the study of the spatial incidence of social pathologies similar to the Watts map analysis illustrated above has recently been demonstrated by the landscape architect Ian McHarg (1969, 187-95). He was interested in "the unity of physical, social and mental health" and their identification with specific social and physical environments in Philadelphia.

Data on the incidence of eight *physical diseases* were compiled and mapped for various areas of the city: included were heart disease, tuberculosis, diabetes, syphilis, cirrhosis of the liver, amoebic dysentery, bacillary dysentery, and salmonellosis. Nine *social diseases* were similarly treated: these were homicide, suicide, drug addiction, alcoholism, robbery, rape, aggravated assault, juvenile delinquency, and infant mortality. *Mental disease* was measured by general admissions and child admissions to psychiatric facilities. For each of the three general conditions composite maps of their spatial incidence were produced by photographing the superimposition of maps of each individual variable prepared on transparencies shaded in three tones of gray and the three summary maps were then superimposed to produce a final composite map of "The Environments of Health and Pathology for Philadelphia." In all four of the maps the heavier the shading the greater the intensity of the problem conditions. The maps all reveal a similar pattern, with the highest incidence of disease in the innner city and on the south side and the lowest incidences in the northwest and northeast.

When the final map was compiled, comparisons could be made with other conditions. McHarg prepared maps on density, air pollution, patterns of population ethnicity, and the "economic" factors of income, poverty, unemployment, housing quality, overcrowding, and illiteracy. A visual comparison between the maps showed that pathology tended to correspond with population density rather than with poverty.

Finally, McHarg sent teams of students into the city to make a more subjective appraisal. In this, "there was no counting of death or disease, but rather of blocks and neighborhoods to identify where children laughed or did not, the demeanor of policemen, the presence of garbage in the streets, broken glass or overturned automobiles, street trees, playgrounds, parks, defiant scribblings on walls, care, pride, or despair" (McHarg, 1969, 193). A synthesis of these observations was prepared on a map, and was found to correspond "to a considerable degree" with the map of the environments of health and pathology. Thus the subjective perception of environment produced results similar to those derived from numerical data on the incidence of social, physical, and mental diseases.

McHarg's approach provides a useful way of identifying the spatial pattern of variation in social well-being in cities. His range of variables is broader than that usually employed in studies of social ecology, and more concerned with pathologies than the census data normally used in factorial ecology studies. The map overlay technique provides for effective visual display of the results, and should commend itself to the geographer. It has now been computerized (Ward, Grant and Chapman, 1970).

Experiments with this technique have been conducted in a pilot study of the "quality of life" in Gainesville, Florida (Dickinson, Gray and Smith, 1972). Data on seventeen variables were compiled to measure the five general criteria of housing quality, home and family life, social order (crime), health, and poverty and welfare. Under each of these headings variables were standardized to a scale of 0 to 100 and then summed to

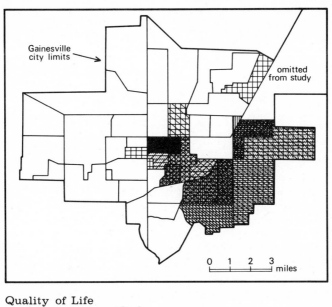

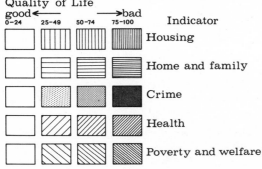

Figure 4.3 The "Quality of Life" in Gainesville, Florida, as shown by the
superimposition of patterns of five general criteria. (Source of data:
Dickinson, Gray and Smith, 1972, Figure 2.)

produce five composite social indicators. A map-overlay application is
illustrated in Figure 4.3, where the areas of coincidence of poor
conditions stand out as heavily shaded. They correspond closely with the
black residential districts.

The McHarg technique enables city social problem areas to be highlighted by a simple graphic method consistent with geographical tradition. For greater precision there are alternative numerical methods, as
will be shown in Chapter 9. But before further discussion of techniques
some more specific conceptual foundations for social indicators research
must be laid. This is the task of the next two chapters.

REFERENCES CITED

Abler, R., Adams, J. S. and Gould, P. (1971), *Spatial Organization: The Geographer's View of the World*, Prentice-Hall, Englewood Cliffs, N.J.

Banfield, E. C. (1968), "Rioting Mainly for Fun and Profit," in J. Q. Wilson, ed., *The Metropolitan Enigma*, Harvard University Press, Cambridge, Mass., pp. 312-341.

Bell, W. (1953), "The Social Areas of the San Francisco Bay Region," *American Sociological Review*, 18, pp. 29-47.

_____ (1955), "Economic, Family and Ethnic Status: An Empirical Test," *American Sociological Review*, 20, pp. 45-52.

Berry, B. J. L., ed. (1971), *Comparative Factorial Ecology*, Supplement to *Economic Geography*, 47, No. 2, Clark University, Worcester, Mass.

Brown, L. A. and Horton, F. E. (1970), "Social Area Change: An Empirical Analysis," *Urban Studies*, 7, pp. 271-288.

Castle, J. M. and Gittus, E. (1957), "The Distribution of Social Defects in Liverpool," *Sociological Review*, 5, pp. 43-64.

Clark, R. (1970), *Crime in America: Observations on its Nature, Causes, Prevention and Control*, Simon and Schuster, New York, pp. 56-67.

Dickinson, J. C., Gray, R. J. and Smith, D. M. (1972), "The Quality of Life in Gainesville, Florida: An Application of Territorial Social Indicators," *Southeastern Geographer*, 12.

DuPont, R. L. (1971), *Profile of a Heroin Addiction Epidemic and an Initial Treatment Response*, Narcotics Treatment Administration, Government of the District of Columbia (mimeo).

Faris, E. L. R. and Dunham, H. W. (1939), *Mental Disorders in Urban Areas*, University of Chicago Press, Chicago.

Giggs, J. A. (1970), "Socially Disorganized Areas in Barry: A Multivariate Approach," in H. Carter and W. K. D. Davies, eds., *Urban Essays: Studies in the Geography of Wales*, Longmans, London, pp. 101-143.

Gronholm, L. (1960), "The Ecology of Social Disorganization in Helsinki," *Acta Sociologica*, 5, pp. 31-41.

Hawley, A. H. and Duncan, O. D. (1957), "Social Area Analysis: A Critical Appraisal," *Land Economics*, 33, pp. 337-345.

Hoyt, H. (1933), *One Hundred Years of Land Values in Chicago*, University of Chicago Press, Chicago.

_____ (1939), *The Structure and Growth of Residential Neighborhoods in American Cities*, USGPO, Washington, D.C.

Jakle, J. A. (1970), *The Spatial Dimensions of Social Organization: A Selected Bibliography for Urban Social Geography*, Council of Planning Librarians, Exchange Bibliography No. 118, Monticello, Ill.

Lessing, L. (1968), "Systems Engineering Invades the City," *Fortune*, 77 (Jan. 1968), pp. 154-157.

Lind, A. W. (1930), "Some Ecological Patterns of Community Disorganization in Honolulu," *American Journal of Sociology*, 36, pp. 206-220.

Lottier, S. (1938), "Distribution of Criminal Offences in Metropolitan Regions," *Journal of Criminal Law and Criminology*, 29, pp. 37-50.

McHarg, I. L. (1969), *Design with Nature*, The Natural History Press, New York, pp. 187-195.

Michelson, W. H. (1970), *Man and his Urban Environment: A Sociological Approach*, Addison-Wesley, Reading, Mass.

Murdie, R. A. (1969), *Factorial Ecology of Metropolitan Chicago 1951-1961*, Research Paper No. 116, Dept. of Geography, University of Chicago.

Park, R. E., Burgess, E. W., and McKenzie, R. D. (1925), *The City*, University of Chicago Press, Chicago.

Rees, P. H. (1970), "Concepts of Social Space: Toward an Urban Social Geography," in B. J. L. Berry and F. Horton, eds., *Geographical Perspectives on Urban Systems*, Prentice-Hall, Englewood Cliffs, N.J., pp. 306-394.

_____ (1972), "Problems of Classifying Subareas within Cities," in B. J. L. Berry, ed., *City Classification Handbook*, John Wiley, New York, pp. 265-330.

Robson, B. T. (1969), *Urban Analysis: A Study of City Structure*, Cambridge University Press, Cambridge.

Schmid, C. F. (1960), "Urban Crime Areas," Parts I and II, *American Sociological Review*, 25, pp. 527-542, 655-678.

Schmitt, R. C. (1960), "Density, Health and Social Organization," *Journal of the American Institute of Planners*, 32, pp. 38-40.

Schnore, L. (1965), "On the Spatial Structure of Cities in the Two Americas," in P. M. Hauser and L. Schnore, eds., *A Study of Urbanization*, John Wiley, New York, pp. 347-398.

Shaw, C. R. and McKay, H.D. (1942), *Juvenile Delinquency and Urban Areas*, University of Chicago Press, Chicago. Reprinted 1969.

Shevky, E. and Bell, W. (1955), *Social Area Analysis: Theory, Illustrative Application, and Computational Procedures*, Stanford University Press, Stanford.

_____ and Williams, M. (1949), *The Social Areas of Los Angeles: Analysis and Typology*, University of California Press, Berkeley and Los Angeles.

Smith, D. M. (1972), "Crime Rates as Territorial Social Indicators," Paper read at the 68th Annual Meeting of the Association of American Geographers, Kansas City (mineo).

Theodorson, G. A. (1961), *Studies in Social Ecology*, Harper and Row, New York.

Timms, D. W. G. (1965), "The Spatial Distribution of Social Deviants in Luton, England," *Australia and New Zealand Journal of Sociology*, 1, pp. 38-52.

U.S. Office of Economic Opportunity (1966), *Maps of Major Concentrations of Poverty in Standard Metropolitan Statistical Areas of 250,000 or More Population*, 3 Vols., USGPO, Washington, D.C.

U.S. Department of Commerce, Bureau of the Census (1967), *Poverty Areas in the 100 Largest Metropolitan Areas*, Supplementary Report PC (S1) - 54, *U.S. Census of Population*, USGPO, Washington, D.C.

Ward, W. S., Grant, D. P. and Chapman, A. J. (1970), *A PL/I Program for Architectural and Planning Space Allocation*, School of Architecture, California State Polytechnic College, San Louis Obispo (mimeo).

Wolfgang, M. E. (1968), "Urban Crime," in J. Q. Wilson, ed., *The Metropolitan Enigma*, Harvard University Press, Cambridge, Mass., pp. 270-311.

CHAPTER 5

THE SOCIAL INDICATORS MOVEMENT

The inadequacy of information relating to social well-being has been a recurrent theme throughout this book thus far. The gradual recognition of this situation in academic and government circles in recent years has led to what may be referred to as "the social indicators movement." Alternatively described as "social accounting," "social reporting," or "monitoring social change," the development of social indicators involves the measurement of social conditions as they vary in time and space. A basic proposition of this movement is that we should be as well informed about the nature and performance of the social system as we are about the economic system.

Background and History

Recent years have seen a marked shift of public attention away from economic affairs and towards the social state of the nation. No one can be in doubt that social problems are now a matter of great national concern, even if the degree of national dedication to their solution may be frequently in question. But the development of social statistics has failed to keep up with this concern. And the comparatively well-developed systems of economic statistics mean that national performance is still measured mainly in economic terms.

This point has been made very clearly by one of the leaders of the social indicators movement (Gross, 1966b, 167):

> Economic statistics, as a whole, emphasize the monetary value of goods and services. By so doing, they tend to discriminate against nonmonetary values and against public services for which costs invariably serve as surrogates for output value. Because figures on health and life expectancy are not directly incorporated in national accounts, progress in these areas may be seriously ignored, either in formulating goals or in evaluating performance.

Gross argues that national economic accounting has promoted a "new Philistinism"—an approach to life based on the principle of using monetary units as the common denominator of all that is important. This is expressed in such things as cost-benefit analysis in which no benefits that cannot be given dollar values are included, econometricians operating on the "ludicrous premise" of a single-valued objective welfare function by which alternative courses of action can be judged, and the "pathetic effort in the United States to debate policies for the 'Great Society' and the 'quality of life' on the basis of concepts developed decades ago to fight depression and provide minimum material sustenance for the population" (Gross, 1966b, 168).

Much of the recent interest in social indicators has been connected with the proposal for a regular national social report. This idea is generally said to have begun in 1929, with President Hoover's Committee on Social Trends. Its report, *Recent Social Trends in the United States* (1933), was an attempt to analyze social factors likely to have a bearing on public policy in the second third of the century. However, very little progress was made in regular social reporting until the very end of that period. Between 1959 and 1966 the publication of *HEW Indicators* and *HEW Trends* represented a small step towards expanding the available social statistics, although the indicators used were rather conventional. Then, within a short period, came four books on the need for social reporting and the many problems involved—a NASA sponsored study edited by Bauer (1966), a short volume by Gross (1966a) for the London-based Tavistock Institute (this was largely reproduced in Bauer, 1966), the results of a Russell Sage Foundation project edited by Sheldon and Moore (1968), and a reprint of two special issues of the *Annals of the American Academy of Political and Social Science* (Gross, 1969). The past five years have also seen a spate of papers on social indicators by sociologists, political scientists, and economists, many of which are listed in Agoc (1970) and McVeigh (1971).

The first thrust of the social indicators movement culminated in the publication by HEW of *Toward a Social Report* in the last days of the Johnson Administration. This represented the first attempt to produce a social equivalent of the annual Economic Reports, and provided a broad if relatively brief review of the state of the nation on a wide range of social conditions. The Nixon Administration committed itself to annual reporting on social goals and indicators but whatever progress may have been made has not been publicized except for the National Goals Research Staff (1970). Congressional interest is reflected in a bill entitled "The Full Opportunity and National Goals and Priorities Act" introduced by Senator Walter Mondale (1971), passage of which would promote great improvements in national social reporting.

The social indicators movement in the United States has had its parallel in Great Britain (Moser, 1970; Shonfield and Shaw, 1972). There has been considerable government interest, expressed in the publication of the new annual statistical report, *Social Trends*. The first issue of *Social Trends* (Central Statistical Office, 1970) resembles *Toward a Social Report* in its coverage, though it is more strictly a statistical document than the largely narrative HEW publication.

Despite the progress in social reporting represented by these two documents, there are many difficulties of a technical and conceptual nature yet to be resolved in this area. As in any movement still in its infancy, there is much uncertainty as to just how the job should be done. Some of the leading issues are examined below.

Social Indicators and Social Systems Modeling

The first question, of course, is, "What is a social indicator?" The simplest definition is probably the one in *Toward a Social Report* (U.S. Department of Health, Education and Welfare, 1969, 97):

> A social indicator, as the term is used here, may be defined to be a statistic of direct normative interest which facilitated concise, comprehensive and balanced judgement about the condition of major aspects of a society. It is in all cases a direct measure of welfare and is subject to the interpretation that, if it changes in the "right" direction, while other things remain equal, things have gotten better, or people are "better off."

Thus statistics on the number of doctors or policemen are not strictly social indicators, as an increase in their number does not necessarily increase human welfare by reducing illness or crime. True social indicators in these areas would be direct measures of health and criminal activity, such as years of healthy life expectancy and monetary losses through crime. As is pointed out in *Toward a Social Report,* this definition immediately excludes a large part of existing social statistics, since they are records of public expenditure on social programs the impact or output of which cannot necessarily be measured by dollars of input.

Some writers add other necessary defining characteristics of a social indicator. These are "that it must be part of a coherent system of socio-economic measurement that can facilitate comprehensive and balanced judgement about the condition of major aspects of a society" (Olson, 1969, 339), that "it is normally used to describe the condition of a single element, factor, or the like, which is part of a complex interrelated system" (Perloff, 1969, 20), or that it is "a component (i.e., a parameter or variable) in a sociological model of a social system or some segment thereof" (Land, 1970, 35). And Culyer, Lavers and Williams (1972) make a useful distinction between indicators of the present condition or state, indicators of the gap between the existing and desired state (i.e., "need"), and indicators of the effectiveness of programs designed to close the gap.

In short, social indicators should ideally (1) measure the state of and changes over time in (2) major aspects or dimension of (3) social conditions that can be judged normatively, as (4) part of a comprehensive and interrelated set of such measures embedded in a social model, and (5) their compilation and use should be related to public policy goals.

Some enormous conceptual questions are raised by this statement. They center around social systems modeling, or the selection of the conditions to be monitored and the way in which they are related to one

THE SOCIAL INDICATORS MOVEMENT 55

another. Again, members of the social indicators movement are accustomed to looking, almost enviously, into the field of economics, where there is a reasonable consensus on a model of the economic system that enables economists to specify the set of interrelated variables that they feel it necessary to measure (Bauer, 1968, 241). Sociology is not in the same position: "There exist no 'social' models that, like our present economic models, identify what parameters are 'relevant' or 'significant' " (Springer, 1970, 5).

The relative success of economics in modeling a national economic system has raised the question of whether the social system might be dealt with in the same general framework. An economist who had a major hand in *Toward a Social Report* says that "existing economic indicators, and particularly the national income accounts, do in fact provide a paradigm that can be used to help guide the development of better social statistics" (Olson, 1969, 338). This had led to the notion of social accounts, or "policy accounts" as Olson (1969, 346) prefers to call them. The objective would be the specification of the system that determines the magnitude of the Gross Social Product, in the same way as economic accounts show the derivation of Gross National (economic) Product.

One possible economic framework for a system of social indicators has been demonstrated by Terleckyj (1970). This is basically an input-output table, in which a list of activities is depicted as contributing to specific "goal output indicators" by means of coefficients similar to the Leontief coefficients in conventional input-output economics. But the fundamental conceptual problem is not solved by this approach—it is merely put off. As Hoffenberg (1970, B-781) has remarked in response to Terleckyj, to proceed to an input-output model involves a theory of production. And even if the equivalent in sociological theory was available, i.e., a scheme that could put the right categories along the two axes of the table, there would be the horrendous empirical problem of arriving at the coefficients to show how much social product a particular activity would input into a particular social goal output category.

Many such approaches being advocated today have their roots in cost-benefit analysis. This is because it is difficult conceptually, and impossible operationally at present, to view the results of a social problem or program with any precision in terms other than money. This is the only common unit that enables the seriousness of, say, alcoholism and drug addiction to be compared, unless we resort to a body count. And it is also the only way of judging the efficiency of alternative programs to alleviate social problems. Perloff (1969) provides an interesting example of the cost-benefit approach applied to a comprehensive framework for evaluating policy measures for the urban environment. Similar to this is the idea of Isard (1969) of building the environment onto the conventional industrial input-output table, as additional rows and columns.

This kind of exploration of alternative accounting frameworks within which the social system might be modeled is likely to go on for some time before any consensus is reached. Bauer (1969, 71-73; 1968, 156) argues that it is possible to look to a consensus on the indicators independent of consensus on a model of society, and that certain parameters can be agreed upon as "important" even if this judgement cannot be made with reference to a general model. The model can emerge as concepts about the nature of society are gradually refined. This seems the only reasonable approach at the moment, and it is on this basis that we can proceed initially to the development of a set of social indicators.

Social Reporting and Social Planning

Before turning to some more specific difficulties in deciding on and developing a set of social indicators, there are some important matters relating to the purpose of the exercise that should be mentioned briefly. These have to do with the public policy application of social accounting and social systems modeling. Social planning, if indeed it exists in the United States in anything other than token form, is not an advanced science. Dyckerman (1967, 248-249) effectively summarizes the situation:

> Social planning is a belated and tentative response of American planners to functional lag. Physical planning, particularly of cities, has been accepted as a legitimate activity at the governmental level for more than half a century. Economic planning, though partial and inconsistent, has been an established part of the governmental scene since the 1930s. Social planning, on the other hand, has been openly recognized only more recently, and then it has proceeded under a cover of confusion which has prevented public debate on its scope and its intentions.

It is an axiom of the social indicators movement that man can, through planning, improve the performance of the social system with respect to the achievement of stated goals. The optimism felt by some, but by no means all, that this kind of public intervention can be an *effective* instrument of desired social change, comes in part from the successful application of modern techniques of managerial rationality to the operation of other complex systems like business corporations. There is much current interest in the extension of the planning-programming-budgeting system (PPBS) into the social policy arena (Rivlin, 1971, 1-8).

The ideal is instructive in pointing to the main problems of this approach. Ideally, societal goals or objectives would be set up that would involve the maximization of some quantitative indicator, or set of indicators, embodying all the variables and elements impinging on social well-being, or more generally on the quality of the good life. Then the functional societal mechanism or system that gives rise to the magnitude of these conditions would be identified, with its variables, parameters and interrelations specified. The system would be closed about a critical set of interacting endogenous variables, and the major exogenous variables that act as inputs to the system would be distinguished. When loaded with accurate empirical data, and with an appropriate algorithm or calculus for simulating the operation of the system, public policy makers would have the social equivalent to an econometric model simulating the working of an economic system.

Such a model could perform the four-stage process of societal management suggested by Bauer (1969, 70). The stages are: (1) the detection of the state of affairs, or measurement of system outputs; (2) evaluation, or determining whether this is the desired state; (3) diagnosis, or finding the origins of the detected state as it arises from the social causative mechanism; and (4) action to remedy an undesired situation, arrived at from knowledge of the operation of the system and of the inputs to it. This kind of rational societal management can thus monitor the system, design remedial programs, resolve conflicting claims for limited resources by identifying the programs with maximum potential goal impact, and project the alternative "futures" or future social states that will be the consequences of different courses of action.

This is, of course, highly Utopian. To be successful it depends above all on the setting of the appropriate goal or goals, and this is a point of major controversy and debate. There are some who argue that it is difficult to believe that a nation has goals other than a consensus on survival (e.g., Hoffenburg, 1970, B-779). Certainly, survival seems to be no less of an objective in the United States today than in more primitive societies, judging by the concern over pollution and population growth, and by the size of the defense budget. But most social reformers are concerned with goals relating to the more equitable distribution of society's resources, goods and services, based on some conception of social justice. Traditionally, economic objectives are prominent in a nation's goals, and they are likely to remain so if only because the production of a surplus to support social programs requires economic efficiency in a competitive world. The major difficulty appears to be seeing economic goals as means of improving social welfare, rather than as ends in themselves.

The truth is that a society is unlikely to establish a consensus even on such goals as "freedom," "equality," and "justice" unless they are left as undefined abstract concepts. "Politicians and philosophers may speak abstractly of a system's performance in enlarging human happiness or serving the general welfare. Both will often maintain that welfare is best served by actions that enlarge human freedom and opportunity without realizing that both concepts are subject to a wide latitude of definitions" (Gross, 1966b, 213). The definitions come with the design and implementation of public policy, often emerging in the process of public intervention rather than actually guiding social programs and broad social policy. It is difficult to escape the pessimism of Hoffenberg's statement that "a broad consensus is needed for establishing goals, and it is only for an abstract nonoperational future domain that the polity can, *ex ante*, reach a consensus. It is only when the chips are down, and resources must be allocated, that we realize that not everyone is for motherhood and that not everyone loves his mother" (Hoffenberg, 1970, B-779).

Another sad truth is that even in a sophisticated technological society such as that of the United States, the idea of judging the performance of the social system is a relatively new one. We are all sensitive about the spending of our tax dollars, yet seldom do we ask for a cost-benefit accounting of this. As Cohen (1969, 201) remarks of education: "the nation has, year after year, been spending billions of state and local tax dollars on an enterprise without knowing how effective the expenditures are, or even if they are being directed to stated goals." In education and in so many other spheres, the existing supply of statistical information does not support goals analysis for the simple reason that it was not designed for this purpose. In a highly individualistic society where power-block politics prevails, there are many who feel that goal-oriented national planning is impossible except in situations of extreme crisis.

Of course, it is easy to exaggerate the difficulties involved in setting national goals and priorities, and measuring the extent to which they are being achieved. But this should not be a reason for avoiding the challenge, and for perpetuating the existing strategy of "muddling through." Some remarks by Rivlin (1971, 46-47) are very much to the point in this context:

> There is a wide measure of agreement in the nation, if not about final goals, at least about desirable directions of change. The bitter argument that rages among the radical right, the middle, and the new and old left over social action programs is not primarily about the objectives themselves. The real issues are the relative importance of these and other objectives (curing poverty versus preserving self-reliance, for example) and the means of reaching them. Almost all the participants in the argument genuinely want healthier, better-educated citizens, and less poverty. These are not empty slogans. They suggest indicators —a set of measurements—that most people would accept at least with respect to the desired direction of change. Most people believe infant mortality rates should go down, reading levels should go up, and the number of people with low incomes should decline. They are not agreed on what they would give up to achieve these changes, how to achieve them, or which ones are most important.

Thus the discussion inevitably leads to questions of conflicting values, which by definition have no absolute base, and to the alternative political philosophies in which such values are ordered.

Problems in Developing Social Indicators

The absence of a general model of society to serve as a guide to what conditions should be measured and how the information might be structured is certainly a major impediment to the development of a set of social indicators. As Moser (1970) remarks, "nothing more effectively achieves improvements in statistics than the attempt to integrate them into a single framework." Obvious examples would be the research into the accurate identification of input-output coefficients prompted by the development of the Leontief model, and the measurement of local "basic" employment required to run urban land-use models of the Garin-Lowry type. Such models require very specific data, and the need to feed a particular set of numbers into a computer to make a model work is a very effective stimulus to data collection.

However, there are severe problems in the development of a set of social indicators, with or without the guidance of a general model. These are discussed extensively in the recent literature of the social indicators movement (see in particular Biderman, 1966, and Etzioni and Lehman, 1969), but they are common problems in social inquiry that have been recognized for some time. They involve each stage in the process of transforming some grand abstraction into a more specific concept, defining this operationally, and taking measurements on the appropriate conditions.

As was indicated in the previous section, the grand abstractions are most likely to achieve a consensus with respect to societal concern. We can all be in favor of "the dignity of the individual" and so on, without knowing just what it is we favor (Bauer, 1968, 244). It is at this level of abstraction that the derivation of a set of social indicators has to start, and the first problem is thus that of deciding what are the grand ideals that society holds. This, presumably, is where goals originate.

Then comes the task of giving these abstractions more concrete identity in the form of specific concepts. It is here that values really enter the picture, though they will not have been entirely absent from the determination of the grand abstractions. The dignity of the individual, for example, may be conceived of as relating to the degree to which he can maintain his personal privacy, the degree to which he has freedom of economic action, the degree to which he has economic security, and so on. Take the single case of how the dignity of the individual, or individual freedom, should be translated into a concept concerning the use of land: some would argue for the freedom of the individual to use land he owns in any way necessary to realize its highest and best use while others would argue for restrictions on the use of land in order to protect other people from undesirable development near their homes that could impair their quality of life.

The next problem is the one generally termed internal validity, or "the extent of correspondence between a social science concept and its operational definition" (Etzioni and Lehman, 1969, 46). The dignity of the individual can provide an illustration again (Bauer, 1968, 244-245). If this is translated into the concept of economic security it is still subject to a range of interpretations. Should this concept be operationalized as job security, or as funds available at retirement? The study of society and social well-being is replete with concepts of this kind, where there may be a range of alternatives for operational definition. And the nature of the concept can change over time; Bauer (1968, 250) offers the example of the change in the criteria of health from death rate through morbidity to the contemporary concern as to whether people are able to function in their social role.

Finally comes measurement, or the assignment of numbers to the variables that operationally define the concepts. Just as poor operational definition can distort the concept, so poor measurement can change the meaning of the concept as it has been defined, or render it virtually without meaning. A basic problem in social statistics is the total absence of data on certain conditions that may represent the best operational definition of some important social welfare concept. Then there is the question of the accuracy of existing statistics, which tend to take on spurious accuracy when they appear in print to two decimal places. One serious source of inaccuracy is uneven coverage, or the compilation of data on different bases in different areas or at different times. The FBI crime index, for example, watched so carefully as a barometer of criminal activity, has been described as "a statistical monstrosity" (Gross and Springer, 1969, 29); few would believe that Mississippi's relative level of criminality is accurately reflected in this index, and there are good reasons for such suspicion (Biderman, 1966, 111-129). Another problem is that measurement is just as subject to value judgements as other stages in scientific inquiry. This helps to explain the measurement of health care in terms of dollars spent per patient day rather than by suffering alleviated, and the absence of much "white collar" and corporation crime from the FBI index while auto theft is included.

Of the many other problems that might be mentioned here, that of aggregation is of particular importance in developing social indicators in the context of a set of social accounts. If the ultimate aim is to arrive at one or a limited number of general indices of social well-being, it is necessary to add together apples and oranges, or infant deaths and auto thefts. In economic accounting there is the common unit of the dollar that enables the production of steel and haircuts to be compared and aggregated. There is no similar way of adding dead children, psychopaths, and stolen cars, unless it is held that the imputation of monetary value (e.g., a productive life lost, the cost of taking care of a mental defective, or the replacement cost of the stolen automobile) does provide such a means. The inadequacy of this notion has already been implied, in the discussion of "economic Philistinism." As is recognized in *Toward a Social Report* (p. 99), "the 'weights' needed for aggregative indexes of other [than economic] social statistics are not available, except within particular and limited areas." At present the only way to develop them would appear to be through some kind of attitudinal survey in which people would be asked to give numerical weights to different conditions.

Any set of social indices compiled today is thus likely to consist, at least in part, of inaccurate or distorted measures of inadequately defined concepts developed uncertainly from some grand abstraction that it is assumed rather than known that people generally agree on, and with few precise ideas on cause-and-effect mechanisms. In these circumstances, the search for some single summary index of social well-being seems very unwise. A recurring theme through the social indicators literature is that in any event the use of a single remote surrogate for a concept in social science is dangerous, and that a varied set of indicators is more appropriate (e.g., Gross, 1966b, 221; Etzioni and Lehman, 1969, 47). And the desire to establish firm cause-and-effect relationships should not obscure the fact that the discovery of close empirical associations or correlations between social phenomena may be of assistance to policymakers, even if they are not fully understood (Krieger, 1969, 9-10; Shonfield and Shaw, 1972, x-xi). We may not know exactly how aspirin works, but it does cure our headaches.

Thus the present state of knowledge should not constrain us too much, both in developing social indicators and using them in the design of public policy. The hope is that by including in a set of social indicators a range of alternative measures of the same general concept or condition, it should be possible to capture most of what really matters, even if it is not possible to define what matters precisely at present. As with the general model of society, the right sets of numbers for its variables and parameters will have to emerge from research during the course of time. And the full value of such information to the policymaker must be discovered through experience.

REFERENCES CITED

Agoc, C. (1970), "Social Indicators: Selected Readings," *Annals of the American Academy of Political and Social Science*, 388, pp. 127-132.

Bauer, R. A., ed. (1966), *Social Indicators*, MIT Press, Cambridge, Mass.

_____ (1968), "Social Indicators: Or Working in a Society which has Better Social Statistics," in S. Anderson, ed., *Planning for Diversity and Choice*, MIT Press, Cambridge, Mass., pp. 237-250.

_____ (1969), "Societal Feedback," in Gross, ed. (1969), *Social Intelligence for America's Future*, pp. 63-77.

Biderman, A. D. (1966), "Social Indicators and Goals," in Bauer, ed. (1966), *Social Indicators*, pp. 68-153.

Central Statistical Office (1970), *Social Trends*, No. 1, Her Majesty's Stationery Office, London.

Cohen, W. J. (1969), "Education and Learning," in Gross, ed. (1969), *Social Intelligence for America's Future*, pp. 186-219.

Culyer, A. J., Lavers, R. J., and Williams, A. (1972), "Health Indicators," in Schonfield and Shaw, eds. (1972), *Social Indicators and Social Policy*, Heinemann, London, pp. 94-118.

Dyckerman, J. W. (1967), "Societal Goals and Planned Societies," in H. W. Eldredge, ed., *Taming Megalopolis*, Vol. 1, Praeger, New York, pp. 248-267.

Etzioni, A. and Lehman, E. W. (1969), "Some Dangers in 'Valid' Social Measurement," in Gross, ed. (1969), *Social Intelligence for America's Future*, pp. 45-62.

Gross, B. M. (1966a), *The State of the Nation: Social Systems Accounting*, Tavistock Publications, London.

_____ (1966b), "The State of the Nation: Social Systems Accounting," in Bauer, ed. (1966), *Social Indicators*, pp. 154-271.

_____, ed. (1969a), *Social Intelligence for America's Future*, Allyn and Bacon, Boston.

_____ (1969b), "Urban Mapping for 1976 and 2000," *Urban Affairs Quarterly*, 5, pp. 121-142.

_____ and Springer, M. (1969), "Developing Social Intelligence," in Gross, ed. (1969), *Social Intelligence for America's Future*, pp. 3-44.

Hoffenburg, M. (1970), "Comments on 'Measuring Progress Towards Social Goals: Some Possibilities at National and Local Levels,' [Terleckyj, 1970]," *Management Science*, 16, pp. B-779-783.

Isard, W. (1969), "Some Notes on the Linkage of Ecological and Economic Systems," *Papers*, Regional Science Association, 22, pp. 85-96.

Krieger, M. H. (1969), *Social Indicators for the Quality of Individual Life*, Working Paper No. 104, Institute of Urban and Regional Development, University of California, Berkeley.

Land, K. C. (1970), "Social Indicators," in R. B. Smith, ed., *Social Science Methods*, The Free Press, New York (page references are to a mimeographed version).

McVeigh, T. (1971), *Social Indicators: A Bibliography*, Council of Planning Librarians, Exchange Bibliography No. 215, Monticello, Ill.

Mondale, W. (1971), Introduction of "The Full Opportunity and National Goals and Priorities Act," *Congressional Record*, 117, No. 3, Monday Jan. 25, Washington, D.C.

Moser, C. (1970), "Measuring the Quality of Life," *New Society*, Dec. 10, pp. 1042-1043.

National Goals Research Staff (1970), *Toward Balanced Growth: Quantity with Quality*, USGPO, Washington, D.C.

Olson, M. (1969), "Social Indicators and Social Accounts," *Socio-Economic Planning Sciences*, 2, pp. 335-346.

Perloff, H. S. (1969), "A Framework for Dealing with the Urban Environment: Introductory Statement," in H. Perloff, ed., *The Quality of the Urban Environment*, Resources for the Future, Washington, D.C., pp. 3-25.

Rivlin, A. M. (1971), *Systematic Thinking for Social Action*, The Brookings Institution, Washington, D.C.

Sheldon, E. B. and Moore, W. E., eds. (1968), *Indicators of Social Change: Concepts and Measurements*, Russell Sage Foundation, New York.

Shonfield, A. and Shaw, S., eds. (1972), *Social Indicators and Social Policy*, Heinemann, London.

Springer, M. (1970), "Social Indicators, Reports and Accounts: Toward the Management of Society," *Annals of the American Academy of Political and Social Science*, 388, pp. 1-13.

Terleckyj, N. E. (1970), "Measuring Progress Towards Social Goals: Some Possibilities at National and Local Levels," *Management Science*, 16, pp. B-765-778.

U.S. Department of Health, Education and Welfare (1969), *Toward a Social Report*, USGPO, Washington, D.C.

CHAPTER 6

TERRITORIAL SOCIAL INDICATORS

The geographical notion of social well-being as a condition with areal variations, which is the central focus of this book, is precisely analogous to the idea of a set of social indicators relating to sub-areas of the national territory. The term "territorial social indicator" may be used to refer to any indicator of the kind defined in Chapter 5 that relates to a geographical section of the nation. It subsumes the concepts of "local," "regional," "metropolitan," and "urban" indicators, each of which can be regarded as a special category of territorial indicators. All the problems connected with national social indicators are present in the study of the geography of social well-being, together with some additional ones.

The Concept of Territorial Social Indicators

The idea of territorial indicators has been a part of the social indicators movement from the beginning. The proposal for an annual social report by the President and a national system of social accounts appears to have been first made by Gross (1965a, 1965b), who also suggested the possibility of social reports for particular states and metropolitan regions (Springer, 1970, 2). HEW soon initiated research into metropolitan indicators, and there has been considerable interest in the same idea under the heading of *urban* indicators (Perle, 1970c; Urban Institute, 1971). Perle (1970b) has also written on *local* societal indicators. Kamrany and Christakis (1970, 209) have referred to *regional* indicators constructed to measure the trends within a specific region and compare it with a larger geographic area. The most thorough exploration of the idea of territorial indicators appears in the study of Perle (1970a) on social reporting in Michigan.

63

Yet despite all this interest in territorial social indicators, most of the main statements and reports to be published are almost entirely nonspatial in their content. The concern in *Toward a Social Report* and in Britain's *Social Trends* is with aggregate national conditions almost exclusively, and this limitation is also true of most of the general reviews of social reporting. Again, there is a parallel in economic reporting, with its emphasis on national data and the shortage of regional or urban economic accounts.

One of the dangers arising from this is well expressed in the following quotation from Stagner (1970, 61):

> Economic statistics have traditionally been aggregate statistics, and our recent experiences have shown how misleading these can be. For example, Keynesian economics led us to the persuasive view that unemployment can be wiped out by a substantial increase in aggregate demand. In the last eight years, we have seen that a massive increase in demand may result in overtime for skilled workers and moonlighting for clerical employees, while leaving festering pockets of hard-core unemployed men and women in our inner cities and rural slums. We count miles and miles of urban expressways built, and then learn that great masses of inner city residents cannot get to jobs because they have no transportation. We can take pride in the rising curve of output of commodities such as automobiles, and then learn that this increase involves no increase in the number of persons employed in the industry. I submit, therefore, that we must turn to disaggregating our statistics, that we must get away from composite figures for the entire city or state or nation, and start dealing with the realities of human beings.

This is the problem that Gross (1969b, 125) terms "aggregatics," which is "a form of mental acrobatics in which non-spatial, macroguesstimates are juggled in the air without reaching the ground in any territorial entity smaller than the nation itself." He goes on to argue that national goals and indicators often have meaning only if they become ways of referring to more specific goals and indicators that relate to sub-national areas of territory; otherwise, "they may have little more significance than would a Weather Bureau report on today's average national weather."

As was indicated in Chapter 1, the preoccupation with aggregate national conditions hides the local situation where the real problems are to be found. This point has been underscored frequently by Perle who says that what is obviously required, in addition to national social reports, is a set of systems of public social reporting produced by and geared to the specific requirements of states and localities (e.g., Perle, 1970a, 4). Local governments at different levels have responsibility for social programs, and the degree of concern with social problems and the commitment to helping the needy can vary considerably. As Wilson (1969, 5) puts it, "because state and local governments have somewhat autonomous and clearly more dominant roles than the federal government has in providing those public services that have a direct and immediate impact on the quality of life provided the American citizen, it becomes imperative that the concept of social indicators be developed concurrently at all levels of government."

An appreciation of the importance of local conditions is apparent in the introduction to the first issue of Britain's *Social Trends* (Central

Statistical Office, 1970, 5-6) despite its present shortage of sub-national data:

> Disparities between different parts of the UK are important aspects of social conditions and although more extensive use of regional tables would go some way towards illustrating them, variations are often very local in character and are concealed within the regions. One way of dealing with this is by means of maps illustrating for relatively small areas concentrations of special social significance.

Social Trends has two pages of maps out of a total of 181 in its first issue, but this is two more than in *Toward a Social Report.* It is the lack of maps more than any other thing that brings home to a geographer the very limited spatial perspective of the social indicators movement.

Adding Space to the Social Data Matrix

The main reason for this spatial myopia, apart from the lack of geographical training of the sociologists, economists, political scientists, and public administrators from whose ranks the social indicators movement has emerged, is probably that changes over time are the prime concern of social reporting at present. To most people, a set of social indicators should indicate changes in a number of different conditions, from some base year to one or more subsequent years. To put it another way, there is a two-dimensional data matrix, with conditions or variables along the one axis and points or periods in time along the other. To introduce a third dimension is quite formidable to contemplate in view of the difficulties involved in the first two, but it is just this that is required. The third dimension or axis would comprise the set of territorial units into which the nation has been divided for social statistical purposes.

Thinking of a system of social statistics, or territorial social indicators, in the form of a three-dimensional data matrix helps to focus attention on the major practical decisions that a researcher attempting to compile such data has to face. Each axis involves a separate classification decision—how to split up the national territory, how to determine the periodicity of reporting, and how to categorize the particular conditions of concern. How to fill the cells of the matrix when these decisions have been made is the measurement problem.

Deciding on the territorial division of some larger area usually involves a compromise between the ideal from a conceptual point of view and what is practicable from the point of view of data availability. At the macro level, the state is the only practicable unit for compiling data to determine broad regional trends across the entire national territory. Ideally, groups of relatively homogeneous counties representing the social equivalent of State Economic Areas would be preferable, but data could not at present be compiled for such a system. The other macro-level possibility is to compare individual cities, which are more meaningful social units than states, and the availability of some data for cities and/or SMSAs makes this feasible. The third (micro) level comprises subdivisions of individual cities, where there is more flexibility than at the macro level to establish socially significant territorial units for the calculation of indicators, by combining census enumeration districts, blocks, or tracts.

Ultimately, there should be some correspondence between territories defined for social reporting and those used for public policy implementation.

Whatever spatial scale is chosen, certain difficulties will arise from the analysis of spatial data. There is the familiar problem of the "ecological fallacy" of attributing aggregate characteristics of areas to individuals or groups living in them. Then there are problems such as spatial autocorrelation that can complicate statistical analysis. Finally, if data are compiled on a sample basis nationally this may lead to considerable inaccuracies in figures for sub-national territorial units if the sample size is small and if it has not been stratified areally.

The time-period decision is not of concern here inasmuch as research in territorial indicators has not reached the stage at which it is reasonable to attempt to measure temporal change. Establishing variations over geographical space is task enough. However, an aim of temporally static research should be to compile all data from the same point in time, or as near to it as the latest available figures for any variable permit, and to proceed in a way which will enable time-series data to be effectively added in subsequently.

The decision on how to categorize the conditions of concern remains. This was at the heart of the discussion of social systems modeling in Chapter 5 but no conclusions were arrived at with respect to specific sets of variables. This is the problem that must now be faced.

Establishing Criteria of Social Well-being

At the beginning of this book it was suggested that the concept of social well-being is sometimes thought of as synonymous with the quality of life. But it may be preferable to regard it as being at the more concrete or specific end of a continuum of abstraction that descends from human happiness through the concept of the quality of life to social well-being. "Quality of life" implies a rather personalized concept, whereas reference to aggregates of people defined by area of residence more appropriately addresses the welfare of some social group.

Recent research on happiness (Bradburn and Caplovitz, 1965; Bradburn, 1969) has indicated possibilities for the analysis of levels of psychological well-being or self-esteem through survey methods. But it is too early to couch the present research in this framework. This approach cannot be dismissed indefinitely however, even in research with a territorial viewpoint; Stagner (1970) has already proposed a set of "psychological urban indicators" that would focus on the frequency and intensity of satisfaction (or dissatisfaction) with aspects of urban life perceived as important by the inhabitants of the city. Indeed, the use of massive surveys designed to find out what the people themselves think of the quality of their lives and the criteria or conditions impinging on it may be the only way to avoid introducing the biased values of the academicians and government officials concerned professionally with social indicators.

The justification for the approach to be adopted here is mainly a pragmatic one. As was suggested in Chapter 5, although there is no generally accepted model from which a correct set of variables can be derived, there is a large degree of consensus on the conditions that should be improved within a social system. These are subject to the normative interpretation that a change in a certain direction, other conditions remaining the same, is desirable by virtue of this consensus. The rationale is similar to that used by Perle (1970a, 27) in his major work on local indicators: "Rather than adopt a deductive strategy stemming from broad goals and then deriving a large number of components, this study has adopted a much more limited domain based on pragmatic considerations of study areas that have a large measure of public concern and policy significance at the present time." However, any specific operational definition of the concept of social well-being ought eventually to relate to human happiness or the capacity of individuals to realize their perception of the good life, for this is the ultimate criterion for determining whether a society is well or sick.

The degree to which there is a consensus on the conditions of concern can be illustrated by a review of the contents of the literature of the social indicators movement. Ten works have been selected and the significance of the treatment of specific topics assessed by the criteria indicated:

(1) President's Commission on National Goals (1960) — criteria: domestic goal areas.
(2) *World Handbook of Political and Social Indicators* (Russett *et al.,* 1964) — major topical headings.
(3) The Russell Sage Foundation study (Sheldon and Moore, 1968) — chapter headings.
(4) A thesis on human well-being in urban areas (Schneidermeyer, 1968) — categories of human well-being indicators.
(5) The reprint of the *Annals* two volumes on social indicators (Gross, 1969a) — chapter topics.
(6) The *Urban Affairs Annual Review* issue on the quality of urban life (Schmandt and Bloomberg, 1969) — substantive topics.
(7) *Toward a Social Report* (HEW, 1969) — chapter topics.
(8) *Social Trends,* No. 1 (Central Statistical Office, 1970) — section headings.
(9) The input-output accounting framework of Terleckyj (1970) — goal output indicators.
(10) The study of social reporting in Michigan by Perle (1970a) — major categories of indicators.

An assessment was made of the extent to which twenty topics were covered or mentioned as major categories of social well-being or social indicators in these works. Because of overlapping coverage of some topics and conflicting terminology, the results can be expressed only as general impressions rather than as a precise content analysis. There is complete or almost complete agreement on the inclusion of four conditions: income

and wealth, employment, health, and education. There is a broad measure
of agreement on a further four: social status and mobility, public order
and safety, the state of the family, and the living environment. Seven
conditions appeared as major items quite frequently but not in more than
half the works examined: science and technology, participation and
alienation, leisure and recreation, social disorganization (or social
pathologies), the natural environment, access to services, etc., and culture
and the arts. The remaining topics given prominent treatment in no more
than three of the ten sources were production of goods and services,
demographic characteristics, the political process, the mass media, and
religion.

Variations of coverage between the works examined can be partly
attributed to their individual themes or terms of reference. What they had
in common was a concern for the measurement of the social state of
nations. Also, the lack of explicit concern with some criteria in some
sources is explained by their implicit consideration under other headings;

Table 6.1. Coverage of leading social problems in ten selected textbooks

Problems	Total Chapters
Crime and delinquency	15½
Racial and ethnic minority issues	11½
Personal pathologies and social deviance	9½
Poverty and economic problems	9
Family and marriage stability, etc.	8
Urban problems	8
Education	7
Demographic characteristics and population growth	6
Mental illness	5½
Communication and the mass media	5
Physical health and medical care	4½
Alienation and participation	4

Source of data: content of the following books:
Cuber, J. F. *et al.* (1964), *Problems of American Society: Values in Conflict,* Holt, Rinehart
and Winston, New York.
Dentler, R.A. (1967), *Major American Social Problems,* Rand McNally, Chicago.
Dynes, R. R. *et al.* (1964), *Social Problems: Dissensus and Deviation in an Industrial
Society,* Oxford University Press, New York.
Freeman, H. E. and James, W. C. (1970), *Social Problems: Causes and Controls,* Rand
McNally, Chicago.
Gold, H., and Scarpitti, F. R. (1967), *Combatting Social Problems: Techniques of
Intervention,* Holt, Rinehart and Winston, New York.
Horton, P. B. and Leslie, G. R. (1970), *The Sociology of Social Problems,* Fourth Edition,
Appleton-Century-Crofts, New York.
Landis, J. R., ed. (1969), *Current Perspectives on Social Problems,* Second Edition,
Wadsworth, Belmont, Calif.
Lindenfeld, F., ed. (1968), *Radical Perspectives on Social Problems,* MacMillan, London.
McDonagh, E. C. and Simpson, J. E., eds. (1969), *Social Problems: Persistent Challenges,*
Second Edition, Holt, Rinehart and Winston, New York.
Merton, R. K. and Nisbet, R. A., eds. (1965), *Contemporary Social Problems,* Rupert
Hart-Davis, London.

this is the case with participation and alienation, and with social disorganization. Some topics also got substantial treatment in the context of the broader abstractions of equality, justice, social security, and opportunity. Despite these reservations, this survey gives a reasonably accurate indication of the consensus of the social indicators literature.

A similar analysis has been conducted of the coverage of ten textbooks in the field of social problems. This proved simpler than the first analysis because of the greater standardization of treatment, terminology, and objectives within these books. As a rough indication of the aggregate attention given to different topics, a calculation was made of the number of chapters or half-chapters devoted to each topic given at least one chapter's treatment in one of the books. The results are shown in Table 6.1, which lists the twelve leading problem areas. Other problems dealt with less frequently are: the power of vested interests and pressure groups, religion, rural problems, politics and civil liberties, science and technology, leisure and recreation, community problems, military affairs, corruption, old age, disaster, and unrest and dissent. As in the social indicators literature, some problems are dealt with more extensively than is shown here, because of partial treatment in chapters devoted mainly to other topics. But again, some impression of the consensus of concern is revealed.

From the literature on sociology, social indicators, and social problems, it is possible, then, to make some broad consensual statements about social well-being. In a well society people will have incomes adequate for their basic needs of food, clothing, shelter, and a "reasonable" standard of living; people will not live in poverty. The status and dignity of the individual will be respected, and he will be socially and economically mobile. Good quality education and health services will be available to all, and their use will be reflected in a high level of physical and mental health and in an informed populace able to perform their societal roles in a satisfactory manner. People will live in decent houses, in decent neighborhoods, and will enjoy a good quality of physical environment. They will have access to recreational facilities, including culture and the arts, and adequate leisure time in which to enjoy these things. Society will show a low degree of disorganization, with few personal social pathologies, little deviant behavior, low crime incidence, and high public order and safety. The family will be a stable institution, with few broken homes. Individuals will be able to participate in social, economic, and political life and will not be alienated on the basis of race, religion, ethnic origin, or any other cause.

Such a statement begs far more questions than it answers, of course. Almost every word requires definition, clarification, or reservation. In some instances it is merely a case of establishing scientifically what constitutes an income adequate for basic human needs or what constitutes decent housing. But in many others questions of social justice are raised, for only against this higher abstraction can judgements be made as to how the rewards that society has to offer should be distributed between individuals, groups, and territories.

Despite these difficulties, the point has been reached at which some general criteria of territorial social well-being can be listed. These can then serve as a basis for an operational definition that can be used to determine how social well-being varies between territories.

Criteria of Territorial Social Well-being

The general criteria of social well-being suggested above were derived largely from studies of society at a national level. But there is no reason why they should not serve at a more local level. The only difficulties at the sub-national level arise when space or area is implicit in a criterion of social well-being, or when distribution over territories is involved. An example of the former would be access to areas of recreation: acres of public park per inhabitant might be a sensible indicator of access to a certain type of facility in a small city, but the same ratio nationally or for a metropolis would make little sense in isolation from the individual's capacity to get to the parks. Also, quality of environment, by definition, is a local rather than a national condition. A distributive example would be physicians per capita: the national rate means nothing to the inhabitants of a rural area or ghetto without a physician, yet at the other end of the scale the absence of a physician in a given city block would not indicate a maldistribution. Access to public services and many other things that satisfy human needs is a partial function of intervening distance and the individual's capacity, usually financial, to overcome it.

Thus there will be some differences between indicators appropriate at the national level and those used locally. There may also be differences

Table 6.2. General criteria of social well-being

I.	Income, wealth & employment	V.	Social order (or disorganization)
i.	Income and wealth	i.	Personal pathologies
ii.	Employment status	ii.	Family breakdown
iii.	Income supplements	iii.	Crime and delinquency
		vi.	Public order and safety
II.	The living environment		
i.	Housing	VI.	Social Belonging (alienation and participation)
ii.	The neighborhood		
iii.	The physical environment	i.	Democratic participation
III.	Health	ii.	Criminal justice
i.	Physical health	iii.	Segregation
ii.	Mental health	VII.	Recreation and leisure
IV.	Education	i.	Recreation facilities
i.	Achievement	ii.	Culture and the arts
ii.	Duration and quality	iii.	Leisure available

Source: Review of literature on social indicators and social problems.

with changes in the spatial scale; an inter-state analysis might be structured differently from one within a city. But in any event a satisfactory starting point can now be provided. Table 6.2 identifies the major criteria emerging from the previous discussion, with subheadings to clarify their definition.

A few comments on this selection are in order. The importance of income and wealth to social well-being is beyond dispute, for money to pay the price may be a necessary condition for access to such services as health and education, as well as required to provide the basic necessities of life. Income supplements refer to welfare services, unemployment pay, and the like. As Gross (1966, 227) argues, material well-being must be thought of in terms of full command over material resources, and includes income, assets, and public services. Income and wealth are also important because they can purchase personal power, prestige, and status as well as more basic material wants. Employment status is included because it is a source of personal status, dignity, and security as well as a source of income. Because it pervades so many aspects of social well-being, the level and distribution of income is sometimes used as the central feature of welfare definition and analysis (e.g., Merriam, 1968).

Housing is important as one of the basic needs of human beings and also because up to a certain standard it can have bearing on other matters such as physical health and mental well-being. Similarly, the character of the immediate environment or neighborhood is generally thought of as influential on the quality of life and on social behavior. The problems of land, air, and water pollution are reflected in the physical environmental criterion, which relates to the basic objective of survival.

The importance of physical and mental health requires no elaboration. It is vital in itself and has a bearing on earning capacity and things relating to this. Education is important to employment opportunity and social mobility, as well as being thought of conventionally as a necessary condition for enjoyment of certain recreational pursuits. Bradburn and Caplovitz (1965) found education, with employment status, to be one of the two closest correlates of happiness.

The various criteria of social order (disorganization) relate to both the unfortunate state of individuals and to the sickness of society at large. Most of the social problems included here can probably be traced back to inadequate income and employment opportunities and the consequent material deprivation, insecurity, and loss of self-esteem. Perhaps more than any other set of criteria, they measure the basic malfunctioning of a society and a capacity to deal with such problems may be important to a society's survival.

Social belonging criteria cover the degree to which individuals can participate in the democratic process, the extent to which they are treated as full members of society with all its rights and privileges, and the extent to which particular groups may be systematically excluded from certain aspects of life in a society. Such alienation can lead to a lowering of self-esteem and to insecurity, which can bring civil disorder as in the case of racial unrest.

Recreation is a necessary part of the good life and this requires access to the facilities and the time in which to enjoy them. The individual choice of recreation can range from the bar and pool hall to the symphony and museum. In including "culture and the arts" here, the question of what comprises culture and art is deliberately avoided; ideally it should be defined with respect to a prevailing fashion or local life style.

The major items omitted from this list but included in many discussions of social indicators require explanation. Because of the lack of a general model of society, there remains uncertainty as to whether some conditions should be included in sets of social indicators despite the general consensus on many criteria. "Science and technology" appears in most texts on social indicators but has been left out here because it is not judged to be a direct indicator of social well-being. An advanced state of medical science and technology might be indicated by the number of heart transplants achieved, but a better indicator of general health would be whether medical science was affecting mortality and morbidity rates. Science and technology, if it serves a useful societal purpose, should be judged by its capacity to influence more specific conditions of social well-being; it is a means, not an end in itself.

Religious participation is not included because its value as a social indicator is ambiguous at best. Religion presumably satisfies some individual spiritual needs, but high church membership is often associated with extremely un-Christian practices, for example towards racial minorities. Thorndike (1939, 99), in the study of the goodness of American cities cited in Chapter 3, found a negative correlation between church membership and the quality of city life, and suspected that "churches are clubs of estimable people and maintainers of traditional rites and ceremonies rather than powerful forces for human betterment."

Of course, value judgements are involved in any selection of criteria of social well-being that has no absolute base in social theory. The same will be true of the choice of individual variables used to measure these conditions empirically. In defense of the selection made here, all that can really be offered is the consensus argument again and the fact that whatever values have been introduced are probably quite widely held. None of the criteria selected depends on an extreme value position though some involve a degree of humanism which not all would accept.

Further discussion and justification of specific criteria of social well-being are reserved for Chapter 7 where an inter-state analysis is presented.

The Selection of Numerical Indicators

When the criteria of social well-being have been chosen, the measurement problem remains. As has already been suggested, the quality of numerical data available for the development of national social indicators leaves much to be desired, and the difficulties are compounded at a sub-areal level. Given the present state of social statistics, quite a lot of the numerical series that have to be used are not true social indicators in the sense defined in Chapter 5. They are not direct measures of well-being like years of health life or value of property stolen, but indirect surrogates like physicians per capita and crime incidence indices.

There can be different kinds of numerical series, whether for true indicators or surrogates. Kamrany and Christakis (1970, 211) recognize three kinds of "regional" indicators: absolute indicators, relative indicators, and autonomous indicators. An absolute indicator is one where there is a scientifically established maximum or minimum level for a certain condition, like the minimum requirements for clean air or the minimum income needed to keep a family of four out of poverty. The social indicator would measure the degree to which these conditions are met in a set of territories. Relative indicators have no such limits or optima but simply measure the relative position of communities by things like crime rates, per capita income, and so forth. The autonomous indicators refer to conditions specific to particular areas or regions that may not be of interest in every territory: for example, the conditions of the Mexican-American population might be a subject for social indicators in Los Angeles but not in Pittsburgh.

For certain conditions, a careful choice has to be made between an absolute and a relative indicator when there are data which offer both alternatives. There are considerable conceptual merits to the minimum-acceptable-standard approach because it is one way of accommodating principles of distributive justice holding that societal rewards should be distributed according to some criteria such as work or need, *subject to* everyone being above a certain level, e.g., that level required for physical survival or comfortable living. In addition, there are some conditions where it is theoretically dubious to argue, in effect, that social well-being is a linear function of some relative indicator. Housing would be an example: above a certain standard of housing, which would include decent plumbing and other facilities, the quality or value of housing appears to have little bearing on human conditions in most respects (see Michelson, 1970, 151-2) though it may influence personal status and self-esteem.

Clearly, relative indicators are easier to find than absolute indicators. The latter involve research over and above that needed to determine aggregate or average individual conditions and also require judgement as to what constitutes a "reasonable" or acceptable minimum standard if the criteria goes beyond physical survival. Thus the data available at present offer no choice but to use relative indicators for most conditions. Among the problems arising from this approach is an implicit value bias, for to use average or median income, for example, rather than proportion below the poverty level or the range or variance in personal incomes implies that the general level of income is more important than its distribution. Deciding on the appropriate goal or desired state is a necessary prerequisite to determining the required numerical indicator.

Outlines of a Simple Mathematical Model

As a conclusion to this chapter, some outlines of a model of territorial social well-being will be suggested. This will be done in simple mathematical terms to provide a bridge between the rather general discussion of social indicators and the case studies to come. Some sort of specific framework of this kind is necessary to structure any empirical investigation guided by a rather abstract concept.

The starting point is the individual member of society. Assume that he (or she) has a set of expectations as to the way life should be, or alternatively a set of needs, and that the personal sense of well-bing is determined by the difference between this and a set of perceptions as to the way things actually are. If $O(1,2,...,i...m)$ is the observed state on various conditions or aspects of life, and $E(1,2,...,i...m)$ the expectations, and if unit linear payoffs between the individual conditions are assumed, then the overall level of well-being (B) of any individual (j) could be expressed as:

$$B_j = (O_{1j} - E_{1j}) + (O_{2j} - E_{2j}) + \cdots + (O_{ij} - E_{ij}) + \cdots + (O_{mj} - E_{mj})$$

or:
$$B_j = \sum_{i=1}^{m} (O_{ij} - E_{ij}) \tag{1}$$

For all the individual (n) living in a given territory, the aggregate social well being (S) would be:

$$S = \sum_{j=1}^{n} \sum_{i=1}^{m} (O_{ij} - E_{ij}). \tag{2}$$

to which might be added a term to express the effect of human interaction and the fact that group social well-being may be more (or less) than the sum of the well-being of its individual members considered in isolation.

Figure 6.1 suggests some elements of the system within which levels of well-being are determined. The individual's conditions or observed states are shown to derive from the general state of the social system, and his needs or expected states come from personal knowledge of life (including cultural predispositions) and whatever concepts are suggested by national ideals of justice, equality, and so on. The interaction of individuals and the aggregation of their personal experiences produces the group social well-being. Extending the model into the policy field, the overall level of social well-being, when related to national ideals, may stimulate social policy and remedial programs which affect the state of the system and level of the individual. Innovations in social policy (e.g., the "War on Poverty") may raise expectations but this and a number of other possible relationships are excluded from the simplified presentation in Figure 6.1.

To take measurements on social well-being conceived in this way would obviously involve large-scale survey research. But until appropriate instruments are developed and applied, some alternative approach to the extensive monitoring of individual experience has to be adopted. At present the development of territorial social indicators must rely heavily on some aggregate measures of (or surrogates for) the individual or group condition with respect to the various criteria of well-being. The focus is thus on what is termed O in Figure 6.1, for some territorial measurements on this do exist whereas nothing precise is known about individual expectation as a spatial variable. If O relates to such conditions as income, education, and health (as listed in Table 6.2), then the levels of O can be thought of as outputs of some subsystem within the wider social system.

Education may serve as an illustration. The output of an educational system may be measured by student scores in various tests and, when

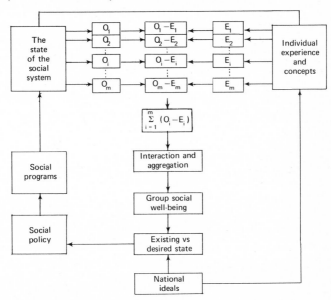

Figure 6.1 A model of the determination of individual well-being.

averaged or aggregated for people living in a given area, these can be regarded as territorial indicator of social well-being on the assumption that educational achievement matters as a means of access to the good life. The actual level of educational achievement (O_E) is likely to be some function of the inputs to the system, for example expenditures on the physical plant (P), on curriculum development (C) and on teacher training (T), i.e.,

$$O_E = f(I_P, I_C, I_T).$$

To accommodate the effect of other variables known to influence educational achievement, such as family socio-economic status (F), other terms must be added, e.g.,

$$O_E = f(I_P, I_C, I_T), f(F).$$

This expression is a simplified shorthand description of the system determining the magnitude of the education indicator of a group of people defined by their place of residence.

The model may be generalized for any social system (or subsystem), as follows:

$$O_i = f(I_{i1}, I_{i2}, ..., I_{ik}),\tag{3}$$

where: O_i is the output of the system i,

$\quad I_i$ (1, 2, ..., k) are the inputs to the system, including those which are outputs of other systems, and

$\quad f$ means "some function of."

The wider social system is made up of various subsystems of this kind. In Figure 6.2 an attempt has been made to illustrate this diagrammatically, showing how each subsystem has its inputs in the form of investments and interaction with other subsystems. These combine in some functional mechanism to produce a set of outputs. Insofar as the inputs and functional relationships vary between territories, so will the level of output. Finally, these social outputs can be thought of as transformed, weighted, and combined to produce the overall territorial level of social well-being (S). Identifying the magnitude of S as it varies spatially is the focus of the research towards which this inquiry is directed.

A similar "heuristic model" of society is suggested in a HEW report on master social indicators (U.S. Office of Education, 1969). It is divided into two parallel and interacting parts, representing respectively the social system and the individual. Both parts progress through a series of levels from very specific indicators of minor sub-system performance to more global measures, finally converging on "the general good." Figure 6.2 can be thought of as representing just one level of the sub-system determining territorial social well-being with respect to the general good.

The scheme suggested in Figure 6.2 is, of course, highly idealistic. But it does provide a reminder of the major problems facing the social system

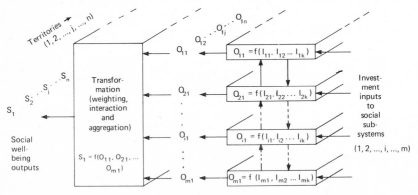

Figure 6.2 Some elements of a model of a social system.

model builder. These are the empirical identifications of the variables, parameters, and relationships involved in the subsystems, i.e. the level of the inputs, the social "production coefficients" which relate inputs to outputs, and the nature of the functions.

Figure 6.2 also helps to emphasize that the territorial level or levels of social well-being are the output or outputs of various interconnected social subsystems. How these outputs can be transformed into comprehensive measures of well-being, or general social indicators, is another major research question. But whereas in the present book the identification of the causal mechanisms behind the outputs is not considered, this transformation problem cannot be avoided. The level of social well-being in any territory can be thought of as some function of the output of the various social subsystems in that territory, i.e.,

$$S_j = f(O_{1j}, O_{2j}, ..., O_{mj}) \qquad\qquad (4)$$

where the output measures are reasonable surrogates for the collective individual experience of the people. In order to develop territorial social indicators from numerous output measures, some assumption has to be made as to the nature of this functional relationship. Various alternatives are demonstrated in the studies which follow, where sets of indicators are developed from information on wide ranges of social conditions.

REFERENCES CITED

Bradburn, N. M. (1969), *The Structure of Psychological Well-Being*, Aldine, Chicago.
_____ and Caplovitz, D. (1965), *Reports on Happiness—A Pilot Study of Behavior Related to Mental Health*, Aldine, Chicago.
Central Statistical Office (1970), *Social Trends*, No. 1, Her Majesty's Stationery Office, London.
Etzioni, A. and Lehman, E. W. (1969), "Some Dangers in 'Valid' Social Measurement," in Gross, ed. (1969), *Social Intelligence for America's Future*, pp. 45-62.
Gross, B. M. (1965a), "Planning: Let's Not Leave it to the Economist," *Challenge*, Sept., pp. 30-33.
_____ (1965b), "Social State of the Union," *Trans-Action*, Nov.-Dec., pp. 14-17.
_____ (1966), "The State of the Nation: Social Systems Accounting," in Bauer, ed. (1966), *Social Indicators*, pp. 154-271.
_____ , ed. (1969a), *Social Intelligence for America's Future*, Allyn and Bacon, Boston.
_____ (1969b), "Urban Mapping for 1976 and 2000," *Urban Affairs Quarterly*, 5, pp. 121-142.
Kamrany, N. M. and Christakis, A. N. (1970), "Social Indicators in Perspective," *Socio-Economic Planning Sciences*, 4, pp. 207-216.
Merriam, J. C. (1968), "Welfare and its Measurement," in Sheldon and Moore, eds. (1968), *Indicators of Social Change: Concepts and Measurements*, pp. 721-804.
Michelson, W. H. (1970), *Man and his Urban Environment: A Sociological Approach*, Addison-Wesley, Reading, Mass.

Perle, E. D. (1970a), *Social Reporting in Michigan: Problems and Issues*, Office of Planning Coordination, Bureau of Policies and Programs, Technical Report A-37, State of Michigan.
_____ (1970b), "Local Societal Indicators: A Progress Report," *Proceedings of the Social Statistics Section*, American Statistical Association, pp. 114-120.
_____ (1970c), "Editor's Introduction," *Urban Affairs Quarterly*, 6, No. 2, Special Issue on Urban Indicators, pp. 135-143.
President's Commission on National Goals (1960), *Goals for Americans*, Prentice-Hall, Englewood Cliffs, N.J.
Russett, B. M., *et al.* (1964), *World Handbook of Political and Social Indicators*, Yale University Press, New Haven and London.
Schmandt, H. J. and Bloomberg, W. (1969), "The Quality of Urban Life," *Urban Affairs Annual Reviews*, 3, Sage Publications, Beverly Hills, Calif.
Schneidermeyer, M. J. (1968), *The Metropolitan Social Inventory: Procedures for Measuring Human Well-Being In Urban Areas*, Thesis Abstract and Bibliography, Council of Planning Librarians, Exchange Bibliography No. 39, Monticello, Ill.
Sheldon, E. B. and Moore, W. E., eds. (1968), *Indicators of Social Change: Concepts and Measurements*, Russell Sage Foundation, New York.
Springer, M. (1970), "Social Indicators, Reports, and Accounts: Toward the Management of Society," *Annals of the American Academy of Political and Social Science*, 388, pp. 1-13.
Stagner, R. (1970), "Perceptions, Aspirations, Frustrations, and Satisfactions: An Approach to Urban Indicators," *Annals of the American Academy of Political and Social Science*, 388, pp. 59-68.
Terleckyj, N. E. (1970), "Measuring Progress Towards Social Goals: Some Possibilities at National and Local Levels," *Management Science*, 16, pp. B-765-778.
Thorndike, E. L. (1939), *Your City*, Harcourt, Brace and Co., New York.
U.S. Department of Health, Education and Welfare (1969), *Toward a Social Report*, USGPO, Washington, D.C.
U.S. Office of Education (1969), *Toward Master Social Indicators*, Educational Policy Research Center, Research Memorandum 6747-2, Washington, D.C. (mimeo).
Urban Institute, The (1971), "Developing Urban Indicators: Some First Steps," *Search*, 1, No. 3, May-June 1971, Washington, D.C.
Wilson, J. O. (1969), *Quality of Life in the United States: An Excursion into the New Frontier of Socio-Economic Indicators*, Midwest Research Institute, Kansas City, Mo.

CHAPTER 7

AN INTER-STATE ANALYSIS

A preliminary attempt has been made to identify areal variations in social well-being at the inter-state level.* As has been indicated already, states are not ideal territorial units for this kind of analysis, for they are not in themselves very significant areas from a social point of view. A particularly unfortunate quality from the perspective of the present study is that characteristics ascribed to entire states can be largely the result of conditions in one or two major cities. However, the use of states can be justified on the grounds that many state programs have an important bearing on social well-being. And in any event, data compiled by states provides the only practicable way of viewing variations in social well-being at a broad regional level at the present time.

The Selection of Criteria and Variables

In recognition of the complex multivariate nature of the concept of social well-being, a wide range of different variables has been selected. They have been chosen so as to represent as closely as possible the general definition of social well-being arrived at in Chapter 6. Of the seven major criteria listed there (Table 6.2), all but one are included in this analysis, the exclusion of Recreation being required by the absence of suitable data. One other, The Living Environment, is included in a restricted form, using quality of housing only, because of the lack of numerical information on the neighborhood and the general physical environment. In all the other cases it is possible to find appropriate if not ideal variables at the state level, though the subheadings under each of the major criteria are not always the same as in Chapter 6 because of data availability. In

*Parts of this chapter originally appeared in an *Antipode* Social Geography monograph (Smith, 1972).

79

general, the variables used here represent a reasonable if not perfect operational formulation of the abstract concept of social well-being.

A total of forty-seven variables have been selected. They are listed in Table 7.1 (in Arabic numerals) under the respective major criteria (upper-case Roman numerals) and sub-headings (lower-case Roman) defining the concept of social well-being that the variables are taken to represent. Some explanation of the selection of the variables is required:

I Income, Wealth, and Employment. The first two variables measure the average level of income (1) and an aspect of income distribution that shows a rough proportion of families in poverty (2). Bank deposits (3), representing savings, provide a measure of wealth. The next three variables relate to employment status: the number of public assistance recipients (4) measures the proportion of people who get economic support from the community (though it does not necessarily give an accurate indication of the number who are not self-supporting and require such assistance), union membership (5) is used as a measure of the status of labor and to some extent of economic security, while white-collar employment (6) is a common measure of occupational status. Five variables concerning the average state levels of income supplement payments are included next: the major source of benefits for retired workers and their dependents (7), the main source of assistance for families in poverty (8), the programs aiding two special categories of disadvantaged persons—disabled (9) and aged (10), and state unemployment insurance (11); these are good measures of general state attitudes towards the needs of the poor and other disadvantaged groups as well as of the available financial supplements to, or substitutes for, earned income and savings. The relatively large number of variables for income, wealth, and employment used here reflects not only the importance of money to provide access to the goods and services that fulfill needs and bring satisfaction, but also the importance of employment and the capacity for self-support as measures of personal status in a society that places high value on economic achievement and self-reliance.

II The Environment. The three variables used here are measures of the general quality of housing, as reflected in monetary value (12), the number of dwellings falling below a critical quality standard (13), and the extent to which homes have certain equipment (14). These variables relate to the immediate living environment, and are also useful surrogates for the general quality of the neighborhood or urban environment, for which there are no direct measures at the state level. No measures of air or water pollution or of more aesthetic aspects of the environment are available.

III Health. This dimension of social well-being is difficult to measure directly, and impossible by such ideal criteria as expectancy of a healthy life. The variables used here are surrogates for the general level of health of the population, and measures of access to medical care facilities. The physical health variables cover malnutrition (15), infant mortality as a generally accepted measure of health levels (16), deaths from tuberculosis which is often associated with poor environmental quality (17), and expenditure per patient in hospital (18) as a measure of the quality of hospital care. Access to medical services includes the availability of hospital beds (19) (somewhat ambiguous as a measure of social well-being because it could indicate the extent of illness needing hospital care), and physicians (20) and dentists (21) in relation to population; these variables reflect effective demand for care offered on a fee-for-service basis. In a system where access to medical care is dependent on capacity to pay, insurance coverage (22) is a measure of individual ability to obtain health-related services. Mental health is measured by the number of inpatients (23) and patient days (24), and also by the hospital expenditures per patient as representative of the quality of care (25). The number of patients can be an ambiguous measure of health levels, particularly for mental health, for high hospitalization rates may be bad because there are so many people sick, good because the sick are being identified as such and treated, or bad because they are not getting cured and released. So the use of the number of mental patients here as a negative measure of social well-being is less easy to justify than is the case with many other variables.

IV Education. This dimension is at least as difficult to measure as health, for although there are many statistical series relating to expenditure on inputs there are very few on educational outputs. Two well-known achievement measures are available at the state level: the illiteracy rate (26) and the rate of failure of military induction mental tests (27). Two variables relating to the duration of the education process, school years completed (28) and college students (29), are included partly as surrogates for achievement and partly on the assumption that exposure to education has societal benefits not necessarily reflected in test performances. The quality of educational services should logically be measured by success in educating people, but the shortage of achievement indicators justifies the inclusion of two measures of level of service, the pupil/teacher ratio (30) and expenditure per pupil (31). The importance of education to social well-being operates in a number of different ways including the improvement of earning capacity and all that goes with it, the bestowal of status and social mobility, and the making known and available to individuals wider ranges of alternatives for the manner in which they arrange their lives.

V Social Disorganization. The first five variables under this heading measure the incidence of social pathologies related to personal deviance, instability, or a behavioral response to a disorganized or stressful social environment. They are the rates of alcoholism (32), narcotics addiction—mainly heroin (33), the two main kinds of venereal diseases (34, 35), and suicide as an escape of last resort (36). In all five cases the figures used, though taken from the best or only official source, are considered unreliable to the extent of substantially underestimating the total national magnitude of these problems, but the relative position of individual states is probably indicated fairly accurately. Family breakdown is another

Table 7.1.   Criteria of social well-being, and variables used in state analysis

Criteria and Variables	Direction	Source
I. INCOME, WEALTH AND EMPLOYMENT		
i. *Income and Wealth*		
1. Per capita annual income ($) 1968	+	1
2. Families with annual income less the $3000 (%) 1959	–	2
3. Total bank deposits per capita ($) 1968	+	1
ii. *Employment Status*		
4. Public assistance recipients (% population) 1964	–	2
5. Union members per 1000 non-agricultural employees 1966	+	1
6. White-collar employees (% of total) 1960	+	2
iii. *Income Supplements*		
7. Average monthly benefit for retired workers ($) 1968	+	1
8. Average monthly AFDC payments per family ($) 1968	+	1
9. Average monthly aid to the disabled ($) 1968	+	1
10. Average monthly old age assistance ($) 1968	+	1
11. Average weekly state unemployment benefit ($) 1968	+	1
II. THE ENVIRONMENT		
i. *Housing*		
12. Median value of owner-occupied houses ($) 1960	+	2
13. Houses dilapidated or lacking complete plumbing (%) 1960	–	1
14. Index of home equipment (max. = 600) 1960	+	2
III. HEALTH		
i. *Physical Health*		
15. Households with poor diets (%) 1965	–	1
16. Infant deaths per 10,000 live births 1967	–	3
17. Tuberculosis deaths per million population 1967	–	3
18. Hospital expenses per patient day ($) 1965	+	4
ii. *Access to Medical Care*		
19. Hospital beds per 10,000 population 1967	+	1
20. Physicians per 10,000 population 1967	+	1
21. Dentists per 10,000 population 1967	+	1
22. Persons covered by hospital health insurance (%) 1965	+	1
iii. *Mental Health*		
23. Residents in mental hospitals etc. per 100,000 population, 1966	–	1
24. Patient days in mental hospitals per 1000 population 1965	–	4
25. Mental hospital expenditures per patient day ($) 1965	+	4
IV. EDUCATION		
i. *Achievement*		
26. Illiterates per 1000 population 1960	–	5
27. Draftees failing armed service mental test (%) 1968	–	5
ii. *Duration*		
28. Median school years completed (x 10) 1960	+	1
29. Persons attended college per 1000 population aged 25 or over, 1960	+	1

iii. *Level of Service*

30. Pupils per teacher 1968	–	1
31. Public school expenditures per pupil ($) 1967	+	1

V. SOCIAL DISORGANIZATION
   i. *Personal Pathologies*

32. Alcoholics per 10,000 adults, 1970	–	6
33. Narcotics addicts per 10,000 population 1970	–	7
34. Gonorrhea cases per 100,000 population 1970	–	8
35. Syphilis cases per million population 1970	–	8
36. Suicides per million population 1967	–	3

   ii. *Family Breakdown*

37. Divorces 1966 per 1000 marriages 1968	–	1
38. Husband and wife households (% of total) 1966	+	1

   iii. *Crime and Safety*

39. Crimes of violence per 100,000 population 1969	–	9
40. Crimes against property per 10,000 population 1969	–	9
41. Motor vehicle accident deaths per million pop. 1967	–	3

VI. ALIENATION AND PARTICIPATION
   i. *Democratic Participation*

42. Eligible voters voting (%) 1964	+	10
43. Registered voters per 100 population of voting age 1968	+	1

   ii. *Criminal Justice*

44. Jail inmates not convicted (%) 1970	–	11
45. Population per lawyer 1966	–	1

   iii. *Racial Segregation*

46. Negroes in schools at least 95% negro 1968	–	1
47. City residential segregation index (max. = 100) 1960	–	12

Note: Direction of measures—a plus sign means that high values are "good" and low are "bad"; a minus sign means the reverse.

Sources of Data:

1. U.S. Dept. of Commerce, Bureau of the Census, *Statistical Abstract of the United States,* 1967, 1968, 1969, 1970, USGPO, Washington, D.C.
2. U.S. Dept. of Commerce, Bureau of the Census, *City and County Data Book,* 1969, USGPO, Washington, D.C.
3. U.S. Dept of Health, Education and Welfare, *Vital Statistics of the United States,* 1967, USGPO, Washington, D.C.
4. U.S. Dept. of Health, Education and Welfare, *State Data and State Rankings in Health, Education and Welfare,* Part 2, *Health, Education and Welfare Trends,* 1966-69, USGPO, Washington, D.C.
5. U.S. Dept of Health, Education and Welfare, *Digest of Educational Statistics,* 1970, USGPO, Washington, D.C.
6. Rutgers University Center of Alcohol Studies, unpublished data.
7. U.S. Dept. of Health, Education and Welfare, Bureau of Narcotics and Dangerous Drugs, Washington, D.C., unpublished data.
8. *Today's VD Control Problem,* 1970, American Social Health Association, New York.
9. U.S. Dept. of Justice, Federal Bureau of Investigation, *Crime in the United States, 1969: Uniform Crime Reports,* 1970, USGPO, Washington, D.C.
10. M. Zitter and D. E. Starsinic, "Estimates of 'Eligible' Voters in Small Areas: Some First Approximations," *Proceedings of the Social Statistics Section,* American Statistical Society, 1966, pp. 368-378.
11. U.S. Dept of Justice, Law Enforcement Assistance Administration, *National Jail Census 1970,* National Criminal Justice Information and Statistical Service, 1971, Washington, D.C.
12. K. E. Taeuber and A. E. Taeuber, *Negroes in Cities,* Aldine, Chicago, 1965.

symptom of social disorganization, and a causal factor in other social problems; it is measured here by the divorce rate (37) and the proportion of husband-and-wife households (38). Crime is represented by the FBI indices for crimes against person (39) and against property (40); although irregularities in reporting introduce some inter-state distortions in these figures, there are no alternative sources for crime statistics of the kind needed for this analysis. Unfortunately, juvenile delinquency cannot be measured by states because the published court records are incomplete. The motor vehicle accident death rate (41) is included as an indicator of personal safety and of societal propensity for violence.

VI Alienation and Participation. Participation in the democratic process is measured by voting rates (42), and voter registration (43) as indicative of the extent to which individuals do and can participate in the election of their officials and representatives. How people are treated when accused of crime has a bearing on alienation and respect for individual freedom and this is measured by the proportion of the jail population unconvicted (44) as representative of the effectiveness of the judicial system in processing accused person, and by population per lawyer (45) as a crude measure of access to (or effective demand for) legal services. Racial segregation is the most obvious form of excluding large groups from the "mainstream" of contemporary American life and this is measured by the extent of school segregation (46) and a residential segregation rate (47) calculated by averaging the rates for major cities in each state.

Given the present shortage of state figures on many important social conditions, this selection of variables represents just about as satisfactory an operational definition of the concept of social well-being developed in the previous chapter as is possible without a major research project to locate or develop the missing series. However, as a set of social indicators these data are inadequate in a number of important respects. Recalling the discussion in Chapter 5, social indicators are supposed to be integrated sets of direct normative measures of major dimensions of social systems compiled with public policy objectives. Many of the variables used here are not *direct measures* of social well-being but surrogates; for example, a higher number of physicians per capita is not necessarily a guarantee of a healthy population, though it makes it more likely than if there were few physicians, and high expenditure on education does not necessarily produce highly educated people. However, practially all the variables are subject to a normative interpretation, as shown by the signs in Table 7.1. The only real problems in this respect appear to be in mental health where a low rate of hospitalization or number of patients may indicate inadequate diagnosis and lack of treatment rather than a low incidence of mental illness; for example, low figures in some southern states would be suspected of underrepresenting the true level of mental disorder, given the high incidence of malnutrition in the young and the known effect of this on mental development.

The data that have been compiled, as a set of numerous individual indices, can hardly be described as an *integrated system* of indicators that

identify *major dimensions* of social well-being. They do represent conditions of general concern but there has been no rigorous theoretical
derivation and by no stretch of the imagination could they be described as
a system of social accounts. Clearly, some manipulation is required before
this kind of matrix of numbers can become a meaningful interpretation of
inter-state variations in social well-being.

A Standard Score Additive Model

The first attempt to derive some general state social indicators to be
demonstrated here involves the transformation of data on individual
variables into some kind of standard scores. This can be achieved in
various ways, including conversion into rankings and the standardization
of the ranges, but the most common method is to use *Z-scores*. The
Z-score is a linear transformation of the original data such that its mean
becomes zero and its standard deviation becomes unity. For observation i
on any variables, the standard score (Z_i) is given by:

$$Z_i = \frac{X_i - \overline{X}}{S}$$

where X_i is the original value for observation i,
$\overline{X}$ is the mean for the variable, and
S is the standard deviation.

Thus when a set of variables are all transformed in this way, two important
parameters of their distributions are equalized, and the units of measurement are eliminated. This enables scores on different variables to be
combined by simple addition, when the signs on those with negative
connotations (i.e., high incidence is "bad") in Table 7.1 are reversed.

A *Standard Score Additive Model* will now be used to develop a
composite social indicator for each of the six major criteria shown in
Table 7.1, and a general indicator including all criteria and variables. The
six criteria indicators require the addition of the Z-scores for the
individual variables taken to measure them. The model is thus:

$$I_j = \sum_{i=1}^{k} Z_{ij}$$

where I_j is the magnitude of the indicator for state j,

Z_{ij} is the standard score on variable i in state j, and
k is the number of variables measuring the criterion in question,
being a subset of the total m variables.

If the results are then expressed as Z-scores, state scores on different
indicators can be directly compared, irrespective of the number of
variables contributing to them. The overall general indicator of social
well-being (S) for any state (j) will be:

$$S_j = \sum_{i=1}^{m} Z_{ij} \quad , \quad \text{or in this case: } \quad S_j = \sum_{i=1}^{47} Z_{ij} \quad .$$

(Alternatively S_j could be the summation of the six I values, which would then weight the six criteria equally.) Again, the result can be transformed back into Z-scores, so that zero indicates average performance and unity (+ or −) represents one standard deviation in either direction.

The conceptual limitations of this additive model should be clear from the discussion in the concluding section of Chapter 6. It requires a gross assumption to define the function which determines the level of social well-being as the summation of standard scores on a set of variables. But in the absence of superior knowledge, the additive model at least provides a starting point for geographical description.

The six sets of indicator scores and the general state indicator are listed in Table 7.2. Figure 7.1 summarizes the geographical patterns of variation on the six indicators by mapping the top and bottom twelve states in each case. Except for Social Disorganization the patterns are very similar, with the bottom states highly concentrated in the South. Alabama, Arkansas, Georgia, Louisiana, Mississippi, North Carolina, South Carolina, and Tennessee all fall in the bottom twelve on each of these five criteria. The top twelve states show a little more variation though Connecticut and Massachusetts appear in all five and Utah, Washington, and Wisconsin are in four of the five. In the Social Disorganization map the concentration of bottom states shifts to the northwestern segment of the nation and includes none of the eight southern states which appear in all the other maps.

Scores on the General Social Well-being indicator are mapped in Figure 7.2. The geographical pattern closely resembles those in five of the six maps in Figure 7.1, with a solid block of "poor" states in the South and the "best" states in the West, the upper Midwest, and the Northeast. In fairness to the South, it should be pointed out that the use of a number of variables relating to income, value of property, and so on, without allowance for the lower cost of living, will somewhat exaggerate the social deprivation in this region though it is unlikely to alter the relative position of southern states very greatly.

The close association between five of the state indicators and the General Social Well-being score is confirmed by correlation analysis. Table 7.3 lists the product moment correlation coefficients (r), and shows that with the exception of Social Disorganization none of the individual indicators have a correlation of less than .88 with General Social Well-being. And none of the five have a correlation of less than .66 with any of the others. So these five criteria tell substantially the same story about the differentiation of the states, as reflected in the General Social Well-being indicator. Social Disorganization varies at the inter-state level largely independent of the other criteria, with all its r values less than .28 (i.e., not significant at p = .05, or the 95% confidence level). The relationship between this indicator and General Social Well-being is virtually nil.

Although no attempt is made here to construct a rigorous explanation for the inter-state patterns of social well-being, correlations with certain other variables are instructive (Table 7.4). Social well-being falls in a fairly regular and predictable manner from north to south ($r = .71$ between S and the latitude of the geographical center of each state), whereas there is

Table 7.2. State social indicators: standard scores on six criteria of social well-being and on a composite indicator

	Income Wealth & Employment	The Environment (Housing)	Health	Education	Social Disorganization	Alienation & Participation	General Social Well-being
Alabama	−1.57	−1.62	−1.89	−1.95	−2.07	0.69	−1.83
Arizona	−0.17	0.18	0.16	0.09	0.07	−1.45	−0.32
Arkansas	−1.68	−2.28	−1.40	−1.46	−1.51	0.02	−1.79
California	1.62	1.37	1.43	0.52	0.67	−2.92	0.65
Colorado	0.40	0.59	1.92	1.40	0.26	−0.68	0.86
Connecticut	1.66	1.65	1.22	0.86	0.76	0.61	1.56
Delaware	0.66	0.94	−0.17	0.69	0.50	−0.12	0.51
Florida	−0.55	−0.06	−0.04	−0.22	−0.76	−1.71	−0.80
Georgia	−1.19	−1.31	−1.21	−1.83	−1.18	−0.58	−1.60
Idaho	−0.06	0.58	0.88	0.44	0.74	0.91	0.70
Illinois	1.16	0.91	0.34	0.22	−0.06	−1.06	0.40
Indiana	0.14	0.23	−0.32	0.02	−0.48	0.21	−0.03
Iowa	0.92	0.45	1.04	0.88	0.72	0.90	1.17
Kansas	0.19	0.48	0.91	0.89	0.24	0.53	0.70
Kentucky	−0.93	−1.51	−0.75	−1.41	−0.71	0.68	−0.95
Louisiana	−1.12	−0.53	−1.12	−1.57	−1.32	−0.43	−1.41
Maine	−0.53	−0.85	−0.42	0.09	1.02	0.76	−0.02
Maryland	0.41	0.59	−0.11	0.46	−0.47	−0.60	0.06
Massachusetts	1.22	0.70	1.03	0.79	1.57	0.04	1.24
Michigan	1.20	0.80	0.28	0.07	−0.05	−0.55	0.48
Minnesota	0.59	0.69	0.79	0.76	1.48	0.70	1.08
Mississippi	−2.67	−2.55	−2.49	−2.41	−2.10	0.49	−2.64
Missouri	0.10	−0.17	0.05	−0.44	0.29	−0.87	−0.21
Montana	0.13	0.21	−0.27	0.93	0.71	−0.19	0.27
Nebraska	−0.10	0.49	0.13	0.64	0.17	0.81	0.40
Nevada	0.77	0.95	0.66	0.53	−0.93	−2.75	−0.15
New Hampshire	0.68	0.05	−0.27	0.40	1.14	1.23	0.78
New Jersey	1.44	1.43	0.08	0.54	0.32	0.14	0.91
New Mexico	−0.67	−0.41	−0.07	−0.09	0.72	−1.12	−0.47
New York	2.18	0.60	0.51	1.23	0.56	−1.89	0.90
N. Carolina	−1.35	−1.60	−1.08	−1.51	−2.14	0.43	−1.53
N. Dakota	−0.04	−0.15	0.05	−0.02	0.58	1.59	0.45
Ohio	0.54	0.95	0.17	0.01	−0.30	0.24	0.36
Oklahoma	−0.58	−0.53	−0.55	0.09	0.02	0.20	−0.34
Oregon	0.30	0.57	1.65	1.39	0.88	−0.60	0.88
Pennsylvania	0.59	0.40	0.23	0.04	−0.36	0.67	0.43
Rhode Island	0.17	0.15	0.65	0.40	1.01	0.37	0.59
S. Carolina	−1.81	−1.95	−1.80	−1.87	−1.74	0.24	−1.97
S. Dakota	−0.62	−0.34	−0.60	0.48	0.48	1.32	0.07
Tennessee	−1.18	−1.10	−0.96	−1.70	−0.89	0.20	−1.25
Texas	−0.54	−0.35	−0.50	−0.60	−1.41	−0.60	−0.88
Utah	−0.10	1.19	2.04	0.50	1.19	1.24	1.21
Vermont	0.07	−0.10	−0.26	0.83	0.09	0.89	0.34
Virginia	−0.44	−0.52	−1.24	−0.52	−1.26	0.50	−0.74
Washington	0.52	0.71	1.53	0.86	1.12	−0.55	0.90
W. Virginia	−0.94	−1.28	−0.93	−1.32	0.44	1.07	−0.66
Wisconsin	0.78	0.85	0.72	0.58	0.91	0.82	1.04
Wyoming	0.39	0.53	−0.03	1.29	0.96	0.17	0.67

Note: The scores on each criterion are the Z-scores of the sum of the Z-scores for the variables listed under that criterion in Table 7.1. The composite score is the Z-score of the sum of the Z-scores for all 47 variables.

no significant trend in a west-east direction. The relationship between social well-being and population density, change, and urbanization is almost

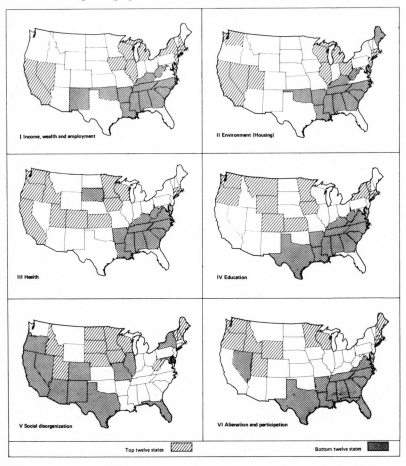

Figure 7.1 The top and bottom states, on six social indicators. (Source of data: Table 7.2.)

uniformly weak, with the exception of a −.54 correlation between population change and Social Disorganization. This latter observation appears to be a case of the classic sociological relationship between unstable population and the incidence of certain pathologies such as high crime, alcoholism, venereal disease, and suicide, which tend to be high in the states with the worst scores on the Social Disorganization indicator (i.e., California, Nevada, New York, and Florida). The proportion of non-whites in the state population is a good negative predictor of social well-being ($r = -.81$ with S), except on the Social Disorganization indicator, which emphasizes the relatively low social well-being of blacks and other racial minorities. Finally, political affiliation (as measured by the 1968 Presidential Election vote) shows the percentage vote for George Wallace to be an effective negative predictor of social well-being, the Humphrey vote a somewhat less efficient positive predictor, and the Nixon vote almost entirely unrelated to state social well-being levels. No cause-and-effect relationships are implied here, though the Wallace vote (largely

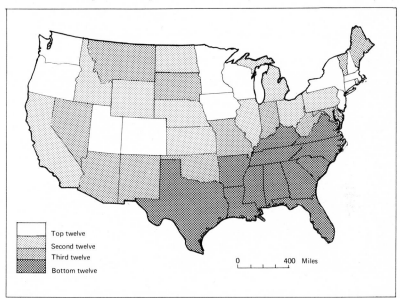

Figure 7.2 State performance on an indicator of General Social Well-being. (Source of data: Table 7.2.)

Table 7.3. Correlation (r) between state social indicators from the standard score additive model

Criteria	I	II	III	IV	V	VI	S
I Income, Wealth and Employment	1.00						
II Environment (Housing)	.91	1.00					
III Health	.76	.85	1.00				
VI Education	.82	.85	.85	1.00			
V Social Disorganization	−.30	−.24	−.20	−.12	1.00		
VI Alienation and Participation	.67	.67	.75	.79	.11	1.00	
General Social Well-being (S)	.88	.90	.88	.92	.05	.87	1.00

Note: The critiera are as defined in Table 7.1 ($r = .28$ is significant at $p = .05$; $r = .36$ is significant at $p = .01$).

southern) was highly correlated with proportion of population non-white ($r = .90$), and it is here that social deprivation is particularly severe. The geographical changes in support for Wallace in the 1972 state primaries along with the new distribution of Democratic and Republican votes shows how transient such relationships can be. However, spatial voting patterns, as expressions of popular attitudes on some social policy issues, are clearly relevant to the geography of social well-being.

Table 7.4. Correlation (r) between state social indicators and other selected variables

Variable	State Social Indicators						
	I	*II*	*III*	*IV*	*V*	*VI*	*S*
1. Distance, west-east	.04	−.14	−.36	−.20	.34	−.13	−.07
2. Distance, south-north	.56	.47	.49	.63	.32	.68	.71
3. Population/sq. mile 1969	.45	.36	.17	.21	−.02	.20	.32
4. Population change (%), 1960-69	.12	.15	.10	.00	−.54	−.29	−.09
5. Urban Population (%), 1960	.17	.21	.18	.15	−.38	.10	.09
6. Non-white population (%), 1960	−.62	−.61	−.72	−.78	−.12	−.83	−.81
7. Humphrey vote (%), 1968	.58	.43	.46	.51	.07	.83	.60
8. Nixon vote, (%) 1968	.02	.07	.08	.08	−.21	.07	.01
9. Wallace vote (%), 1968	−.68	−.61	−.67	−.78	.03	−.77	−.77

The State Social Indicators are as identified in Table 7.2.

An Additive Model with Weighted Variables

In the analysis above, each variable was weighted equally with respect to its contribution to the indicator in question and to the final S-score. An alternative model might give a different weight to each variable, i.e.,

$$S_j = \sum_{i=1}^{m} w_i Z_{ij} \, ,$$

where S_j is social well-being in state j,
Z_{ij} is the standard score on variable i in state j,
w_i is the weighting for variable i, and
m is the number of variables (i.e., 47 in this case).

The critical problem here is arriving at appropriate weightings. There is no theoretical guidance and the intuitive judgement of the individual researcher may do little more than reveal his value preferences. At present, some kind of attitudinal survey seems to be the only way of deriving such weights. The aggregate response to questions concerning the relative importance of different conditions can be interpreted as a measure of general consensus.

As an illustrative experiment in the empirical derivation of weightings each of the fifteen members of an advanced geography class at the

University of Florida was asked to select from Table 7.1 the ten variables which best represented his/her own concept of social well-being. The frequency of selection is taken as a weighting. Per capita income has the highest weight, followed by crimes of violence, households with poor diets, physicians, low income families, and suicides. Only four of the forty-seven variables (tuberculosis deaths, dentists, mental hospital expenditures, and illiterates) were selected by no one. These results of course reflect certain student attitudes and values which will not necessarily be shared by many of the other groups of people whose opinions might have been solicited.

The General Social Well-being indicator from the previous section has been recalculated by multiplying each of the forty-seven sets of Z-scores by the appropriate weight from the student survey. A comparison with the rankings on the indicator calculated from unweighted data shows that there is little change in the ordinal position of the states; only four have a change in rank of more than five places. A rank correlation coefficient (Spearman) of .977 confirms the high degree of similarity between the two indicators. Thus this particular set of weightings makes little difference to state performance on a General Social Well-being indicator, based on a standard score additive model.

A variant on this model would be to include weightings specific to each territory as well as to each variable, i.e.,

$$S_j = \sum_{i=1}^{m} w_{ij} Z_{ij}$$

Thus geographical differences in perception of the relative importance of the individual criteria or variables could be incorporated. This would be a step in the direction of accommodating local characteristics of culture and associated value preferences.

A Principal Components Model

The similarity between the results on five of the six criteria indicators (Table 7.3), and between the general indicator with weighted or unweighted data, is an outcome of the relationships between individual variables. These can be revealed by correlation analysis. The full matrix of coefficients and the more important findings are set down in Smith (1972) and need not be reproduced here. Briefly, most of the variables relating to affluence—income, occupational status, housing, and education—tend to convey a similar general impression while the states perform in a markedly different manner on most of the social disorganization variables. This is what the six indicators developed earlier in this chapter showed. Thus there are strong linkages among certain sets of social conditions viewed at this level of spatial aggregation. Even if the causal mechanisms implied in this cannot yet be clearly interpreted, the incorporation of the empirical relationships within a set of social indicators seems a sensible objective.

Principal components analysis (or factor analysis) has been used for some time to identify the underlying dimensions of variance in large matrices of spatial data. Some applications have already been presented in

Chapters 2, 3, and 4. These techniques offer another alternative approach to the development of territorial social indicators by reducing data on many variables to a small number of sets of composite scores which derive their identity from the intercorrelation between individual conditions. Components analysis is preferred to factor analysis here for the objective is parsimony in data compression, or the extraction of maximum variance, rather than testing for some specific structure. However, there is often little difference between the results of the two, as Wilson (1969, 11) found in his inter-state analysis of quality of life.

Principal components analysis (see footnote on p. 11) produces a new set of variables from the original data. Each component is identified by its loadings (ℓ), or the correlation coefficient between the new variable and the original one. The sum of the product of the appropriate loading and the original score (Z) on each variable gives a score for any observation on any component. If a component is interpreted as measuring a major dimension of social well-being extracted from data on a wide range of social variables, it provides an indicator of the following specification:

$$I_j = \ell_1 Z_{1j} + \ell_2 Z_{2j} + \cdots + \ell_i Z_{ij} + \cdots + \ell_m Z_{mj} \; ,$$

or:
$$I_j = \sum_{i=1}^{m} \ell_i Z_{ij} \; ,$$

where I_j is the magnitude of the indicator in territory j,

        ℓ_i is the loading on variable i for the component in question,

and Z_{ij} is the standard score on variable i in territory j.

The principal components (or factor analysis) model thus provides one possible empirical approach to the problem of weighting individual conditions in a social indicator. It has already been used for this purpose by Wilson (1969, 9-11). The weightings emerge from the interrelationships between the variables as they align themselves into components.

There will be as many components as there were original variables. However, the leading components may account for sufficient of the variance in the original data that they can be used for the classification of territories or for the development of a simple general indicator by themselves. If scores on the leading components can be interpreted unambiguously as indicators of social well-being in a certain direction (i.e., positive scores are "good," negative "bad"), then they can be combined in an additive model as follows:

$$S_j = \sum_{i=1}^{p} w_i I_{ij} \; ,$$

where S_j is general social well-being in territory j,

      I_{ij} is the score on component (or indicator) i for territory j,

      w_i is some weighting of component i,

and the summation is over p components where p is a subset of m. These approaches to the development of territorial social indicators may now be illustrated at the state level.

The results of the principal components analysis are summarized in Table 7.5. One general component well correlated with many of the original variables accounts for almost forty percent of the total variance

Table 7.5. Principal components of social well-being at the state level

Component Number	Component Description	Eigenvalue* (total = 47)	Cumulative Explained Variance (%)
1	General Socio-economic Well-being	18.14	38.56
2	Social Pathology	6.46	52.30
3	Mental Health	5.63	64.28
4	Racial Segregation	1.86	70.22
5	Public Assistance/Unionization	1.74	73.94
6	Social Disruption	1.68	77.49

*The eigenvalue shows the proportion of variance accounted for by the component in question.

Note: First six components from the principal axis solution, without rotation.

and a further two important components together raise this to almost two-thirds. Subsequent components individually add relatively little to the variance accounted for.

The structure of the three leading components, as revealed by the high-loading variables, is shown in Table 7.6. Component 1 loads high (i.e., over .75) on variables representing all the six major criteria of social well-being covered by this analysis except for Social Disorganization. Particularly prominent are variables relating to poverty and affluence (i.e., income levels and income supplement payments), with health and education also well represented. This component is therefore termed *General Socio-economic Well-being*. It is a very general and broadly defined indicator of social well-being accounting for more than three-quarters of the variance in sixteen of the original variables and at least half in all but fifteen of them. High positive scores on this first component indicate a good state of social well-being.

Component 2 is obviously associated with social disorganization, which provides half the variables loading over .50. The prominence of venereal diseases, narcotics addiction, and crime suggests the description of *Social Pathology*. The variables listed in Table 7.6 give the impression that it is largely the social problems of the big cities that this component has identified. High positive scores clearly indicate poor conditions of social well-being on this component, as shown by the signs of the loadings.

Component 3 is more difficult to interpret. The high-loading variables (over .45) listed in the table include a mixture of positive and negative measures (see signs in Table 7.1), as compared with the unanimity of direction shown in the other two components. The first three variables show low mental illness hospitalization associated with high hospital expenditures but the fourth shows these associated with low numbers of hospital beds—a variable working in the same direction as the other three only if it is interpreted as the result of a well population not needing a large number of hospital beds. Other variables in the same direction (i.e., positive = good) are mental hospital expenses and two education indicators. But the remaining four high-loading variables (divorce, suicide, motor vehicle accident deaths, and property crimes)—pathologies reflecting affluence rather than poverty—all appear to be in conflict with the general trend. This component thus depicts a situation in which some aspects of social disorganization are associated with high expenditures on medical care and low mental hospitalization. One possible interpretation is that although good medical care is available, some of the mentally ill do not get treated and this is reflected in social disorganization. But it may be the case that the different characteristics of two distinct groups within the state populations are being revealed. Whatever the interpretation, this

Table 7.6. Structure of the three leading components of social well-being at the state level

COMPONENT 1: *GENERAL SOCIO-ECONOMIC WELL-BEING* (explained variance: 38.56%)

highest loadings:	−.9398 families with income less than $3000
	−.9083 houses dilapidated etc.
	.8951 benefits for retired workers
	.8853 per capita income
	.8651 dentists/10,000 population
	.8556 AFDC payments
	.8086 state unemployment benefit
	.8065 value of owner-occupied houses
	−.7993 households with poor diets
	−.7993 infant deaths
	.7868 public school expenditures
	−.7834 mental test failures
	.7780 eligible voters voting
	.7749 white-collar employees
	.7615 physicians/10,000 population
	.7587 median school years completed

COMPONENT 2: *SOCIAL PATHOLOGY* (explained variance: 13.74%)

highest loadings:	.8384 crimes of violence
	.7236 syphilis cases
	.6719 gonorrhea cases
	.6528 narcotics addicts
	.6422 school segregation
	−.6325 registered voters
	.6043 crimes against property
	.5517 illiteracy
	.5413 tuberculosis deaths
	−.5329 index of home equipment

COMPONENT 3: *MENTAL HEALTH* (explained variance: 11.98%)

highest loadings:	−.8174 patient days in mental hospitals
	.7999 hospital expenses/patient day
	−.7940 residents in mental hospitals etc.
	−.7800 hospital beds/10,000 population
	.6323 divorces
	.5583 suicides
	.4932 mental hospital expenditures/patient days
	.4696 motor vehicle accident deaths
	.4601 crimes against property
	.4568 median school years completed
	.4548 persons attended college

component can be reasonably labeled *Mental Health,* though it is some-what broader than this in its scope. Because of the apparent conflict between variables it seems unwise to regard scores on Component 3 as an unambiguous indicator of social well-being, as is possible with Components 1 and 2.

The other three components included in Table 7.5 have low eigen-values, and a detailed interpretation is not pertinent here. Component 4, *Racial Segregation,* has a loading of almost .6 on the city residential segregation index, followed by .43 on bank deposits, .41 on households with inadequate diet, .36 on the index of home equipment, .28 on school segregation, and almost .28 on gonorrhea. It suggests segregated and deprived black populations juxtaposed with enough affluent people to push bank deposits and home equipment up to quite high levels on average. Component 5, *Public Assistance/Unionization,* has loadings of .62 on the proportion of the population on public assistance and .61 union membership as a proportion of all non-agricultural workers, thus associ-ating two variables that were assumed to operate in opposite directions as measures of social well-being. As with Component 3, the unsatisfactory nature of states as social statistical units may be partially responsible for this apparent conflict but it is also the case that, up to a point, high numbers on public assistance are a positive measure of social well-being because they mean that the needy are getting help that they might be denied in a less generous state. Component 6 loads −.54 on husband-and-wife households, almost .54 on suicide, and .44 on motor vehicle accident deaths. It appears to identify a dimension of social disorganization somewhat different from Component 2, and is called *Social Disruption* for want of a better term.

State scores on the three leading components and rankings on 1 and 2 are listed in Table 7.7. The scores have been standardized and weighted so that their mean is zero and variance equals the eigenvalue and they have then been multiplied by 100 to eliminate the decimal points. The scores on Components 1 and 2 satisfy important criteria of social indicators in that they are normative measures of major dimensions of social well-being.

The geographical pattern of inter-state variations in social well-being may now be considered through maps of the component scores. Scores on Component 1, General Socio-economic Well-being, are mapped in Figure 7.3 (top), where high positive values are "good" and high negative values "bad." The most prominent feature of the map is the concentration of high negative values in the South, in a belt running from Texas to the Virginias. Concentrations of high or relatively high positive scores are found in the central mountain and western states, in the upper Midwest, and in the eastern end of the major manufacturing belt. Part of the Southwest, the Plains, most of the major manufacturing belt, the upper mountain states, northern New England, and Florida, occupy intermediate positions. That this broad dimension of social well-being improves fairly steadily away from the South will come as no surprise, for such a finding was anticipated in all but one of the maps in Figure 7.1 earlier in this chapter. The highest score among the states is for New York, followed by

Table 7.7. State scores on leading components of social well-being, and on a composite social indicator

State	Component 1		Component 2		Component 3	1 & 2	
	Score	Rank	Score	Rank	Score	Score	Rank
Alabama	−784	46	−101	31	− 92	−885	45
Arizona	− 33	30	−173	38	511	−206	35
Arkansas	−722	45	− 18	22	52	−790	43
California	592	4	−388	47	356	204	22
Colorado	407	6	− 20	23	337	387	15
Connecticut	639	2	− 84	30	−135	555	3
Delaware	253	15	− 65	29	−100	188	23
Florida	−154	34	−311	42	259	−465	39
Georgia	−632	43	−269	41	− 54	−901	46
Idaho	63	26	424	2	320	487	8
Illinois	327	10	−313	44	−120	13	29
Indiana	− 17	29	139	16	− 1	123	26
Iowa	227	18	370	4	− 9	597	2
Kansas	125	24	270	10	166	395	14
Kentucky	−485	40	43	20	1	−442	37
Louisiana	−512	41	−340	45	− 16	−852	44
Maine	− 78	32	305	7	−236	227	21
Maryland	184	22	−350	46	22	−166	33
Massachusetts	604	3	−145	35	−281	459	11
Michigan	299	13	−127	32	− 81	172	25
Minnesota	307	11	212	12	−143	519	5
Mississippi	−1128	48	−158	36	− 80	−1286	48
Missouri	16	28	−131	33	− 47	−115	32
Montana	82	25	275	9	139	356	16
Nebraska	48	27	254	11	− 91	302	17
Nevada	251	16	−319	43	450	− 68	30
New Hampshire	208	19	315	6	−271	523	6
New Jersey	469	5	−222	40	−159	247	20
New Mexico	−176	35	46	26	483	−222	36
New York	781	1	−739	48	−505	42	28
North Carolina	−681	44	− 20	24	− 43	−701	42
North Dakota	− 48	31	450	1	−261	402	12
Ohio	155	23	− 46	27	− 18	109	27
Oklahoma	−188	36	82	18	92	−106	31
Oregon	330	8	138	17	217	468	9
Pennsylvania	193	21	− 17	21	−279	176	24
Rhode Island	328	9	− 41	25	−255	286	18
South Carolina	−832	47	−170	37	−183	−1002	47
South Dakota	−154	33	406	3	−212	252	19
Tennessee	−599	42	− 51	28	− 49	−610	41
Texas	−320	38	−216	39	190	−536	40
Utah	266	14	339	5	519	605	1
Vermont	196	20	206	14	−341	402	12
Virginia	−319	37	−131	34	− 89	−450	38
Washington	380	7	80	19	358	460	10
West Virginia	−398	39	209	13	−152	−189	34
Wisconsin	300	12	202	15	−142	502	7
Wyoming	239	17	291	8	− 47	530	4

Note: The scores on each component have been standardized so that mean = 0 and variance = eigenvalue, and then multiplied by 100. The original signs of scores on Component 2 have been reversed to make positive scores "good" and negative scores "bad." Scores on 1 + 2 are subject to rounding errors.

Source: Smith (1972, 43-44).

Connecticut, Massachusetts, and California while the lowest (highest negative) is for Mississippi, followed by South Carolina, Alabama, and Arkansas.

Scores on Component 2, Social Pathology, are shown in the bottom half of Figure 7.3. Now there is an almost continuous belt of negative

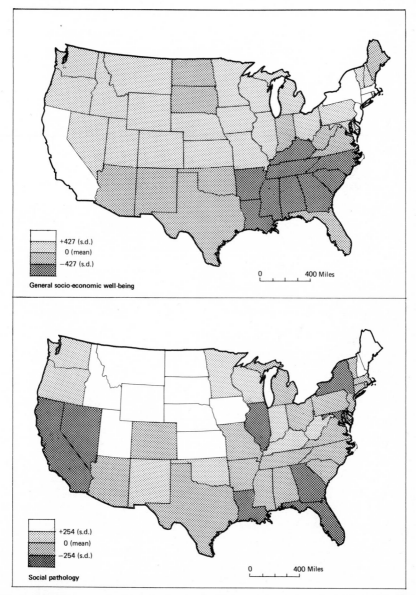

Figure 7.3 State performance on two leading components of social well-being, based on factor scores standardized so that mean = 0 and standard deviation (s.d.) = square root of eigenvalue. (Source: Smith, 1972.)

scores extending from California and Nevada in the West, through the South, and up to New York and southern New England. The highest negative scores are in New York and California—two of the highest positive states on Component 1—followed by Maryland, Louisiana, Nevada, and Florida. These are all states with major cities containing deprived minority populations subject to a high incidence of many social problems. Positive scores appear in a belt from the Northwest to the upper Midwest, in three New England states, and in Indiana-Kentucky-West Virginia. The highest postive scores, indicating the lowest incidence of social pathologies, are in the Dakotas, Idaho, and Iowa—states without major urban concentrations.

Scores on Component 3, though not mapped here, show a very interesting geographical pattern of variation (see Smith, 1972). While the general trend in Components 1 and 2 is for an improvement from south to north, in Component 3 the change is from east to west. Here the highest positive scores (not necessarily "good") are in the Utah, Arizona, New Mexico, and Nevada area of the Southwest where there exist distinctive social groups that include affluent city dwellers, people in retirement, the Mormons, Mexican Americans, and the Indians on the reservations. This social heterogeneity no doubt has a bearing on the performance of these states on Component 3 and on some of the apparent conflict of indicators in the loadings (Table 7.6). The highest negative scores are in the New York-New England area and in the Dakotas. A comparison with the Social Disorganization indicator from the additive model (Figure 7.1) suggests that this component may be picking up some of the problems of the Southwest (e.g., high suicide, alcoholism, and violence) not included in the Social Pathology component mapped in Figure 7.3, and associated with population growth. On balance, the change from east to west seems more likely to be from "good" to "bad" than the reverse.

The final stage in this analysis is an attempt to summarize inter-state variations on the different dimensions of social well-being revealed by the principal components analysis. Because of the ambiguous nature of Component 3, this is based entirely on scores on Components 1 and 2, which together account for more than half of the variance in the original forty-seven variables used to measure social well-being. Two methods are used, the first involving a grouping analysis while the second is based on a summation of component scores.

The result of the grouping analysis is shown in Figure 7.4, where state scores on General Socio-economic Well-being and on Social Pathology are plotted. The stepwise grouping of states according to similarity of social well-being, or proximity on the graph, was terminated with the formation of the four groups shown—A, B, C and D. Each of these groups is distinctively situated with respect to the two leading dimensions of social well-being. Group A includes states with relatively good performance on both General Socio-economic Well-being and Social Pathology; all have positive (i.e., above average) scores on Component 2, and all but three have positive scores on Component 1. The states in Group B do better on General Socio-economic Well-being than on Social Pathology for all have positive scores on Component 1 and negative (below average) scores on Component 2. The states in Group B tend to be highly urban and industrial compared to the generally rural or agricultural character of those in Group A. Both groups occupy roughly the same average position on the good to bad (top right to bottom left) continuum of social well-being. Group C is clearly worse off than A and B with respect to

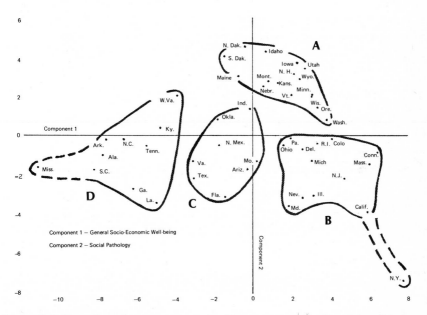

Figure 7.4 Grouping of states on two leading components of social well-being. (Source: Smith, 1972.)

General Socio-economic Well-being, but on average slightly better than B though obviously worse than A on Social Pathology. Group D is very similar to C on Social Pathology, but markedly worse on General Socio-economic Well-being.

Membership of these four groups is mapped in Figure 7.5 (top). Although no contiguity constraint was used in the grouping analysis, as is sometimes done to create spatially continuous regions, a number of clear belts have emerged. The members of Group A form a continuous belt from the Pacific Northwest to the Great Lakes, with an outlier in upper New England. At the other end of the continuum, the members of Group D form a compact block in the South. Group C comprises five contiguous states, with the outlying members of Indiana, Virginia, and Florida to the east. Group C has its main concentration in the major manufacturing belt, with outliers in Colorado and California-Nevada. The clear impression is of a core area of low social well-being in the South, a belt of high social well-being extending across the north of the country from coast to coast, and an intermediate or transitional zone separating them both geographically and socially. The general impression of regional homogeneity with respect to social well-being is interrupted only in the belt from Missouri to Maryland where three of the four groups are represented.

The second summary is provided by simply adding the scores for each state on the first two components. This is justified on the grounds that both sets of scores have been interpreted as unambiguous composite

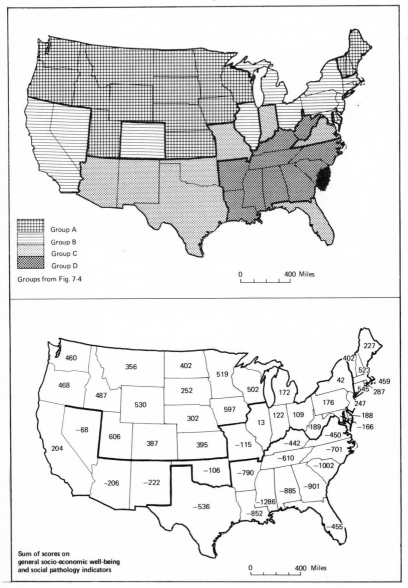

Figure 7.5 Two views of the regional geography of social well-being at the inter-state level, based on scores on the two leading components. (Source: Smith, 1972.)

indicators of social well-being in a certain direction. As the scores are standardized to zero mean and the variance equal to the appropriate component eigenvalue, they will be weighted in the summation in accordance with their share of the explained variance of the original data. The summation of the scores on Components 1 and 2 means that over half the variance in forty-seven original variables can be represented by a single index which may be regarded as a good comprehensive state indicator of social well-being. The state scores and ranks are listed in Table 7.7.

This new set of scores ranges from 606 in Utah to −1286 in Mississippi. They are mapped in Figure 7.5 (bottom), which shows a tendency towards geographical grouping very similar to that shown in the top map. The general impression is of groups of states with similar high or low levels of social well-being, bounded by extreme changes in scores. Thus, for example, the scores change across the southern border of Utah, Colorado, and Kansas by about 800, 600, and 500 respectively. Lines have been drawn on the map to indicate these extreme changes and these can be regarded as boundaries between relatively homogenous regions from the point of view of social well-being. Three major regions can be identified: the belt of states from the Pacific Northwest to the Great Lakes, with its outlier in New England, as the region of high social well-being; the South from Texas to Virginia, as the region of low social well-being; and the transitional zone virtually continuous from California to New York.

The Inter-state Geography of Social Well-being

Three alternative models have been used in this chapter for the development of state social indicators. A fairly distinctive pattern of regional differentiation emerged from the simple summation of standard scores on a wide range of social conditions and the weighting of variables was found to affect the ordering of states very little. Other indicators have now been developed in a principal components analysis and these tend to confirm the earlier results. The rank correlation coefficients (Spearman) between the General Social Well-being indicator derived from summing the unweighted Z-scores (Table 7.2) and the three indicators from the components analysis are as follows:

Component 1: General Socio-economic Well-being   .904
Component 2: Social Pathology   .370
Sum of scores on Components 1 and 2   .914

Thus the order of the states on two of these indicators is correlated with the result of the additive model at a very high level of significance ($p < .001$). The relationship with rankings on the Social Pathology component, though significant at $p = .05$, is much weaker.

There is only one other analysis of inter-state variations in social conditions that is comparable to that attempted here—the study of the quality of life in the United States by Wilson (1969) to which reference was made in Chapter 2. How close were Wilson's results to those of the present analysis? Of the eleven domestic goal areas for which Wilson produced state rankings, only six are relevant here—health and welfare, living conditions, education, democratic process, equality, and status of the individual. Wilson's rankings may be compared to the ranking of states on the two leading components of social well-being and with the rankings on their sum (Table 7.7). The Spearman rank correlation coefficients with the Wilson composite rankings are as follows:

> Component 1: General Socio-economic Well-being   .947
> Component 2: Social Pathology   .121
> Sum of scores on Components 1 and 2   .821

Thus there is a highly significant degree of correspondence ($p < .001$) between the state rankings on six relevant domestic goal areas as measured by Wilson and on the ranking of states according to scores on the General Socio-economic Well-being indicator identified here. The correspondence with rankings on the summed scores is also high ($p < .001$). But the correspondence between the Wilson rankings and those on the Social Pathology indicator is so weak as to be non-significant at the 90% confidence level. The reason for this is very simple: while in the present study great weight was given to the general condition of social disorganization by the inclusion of ten variables in the original selection, the only one that Wilson included in his analysis was a crime index. Otherwise, the results of the two studies are closely similar.

One general conclusion emerges quite clearly. This is the existence of two major independent dimensions of inter-state variation in social well-being. There is a predominant dimension within which relatively high incomes are associated with good housing, high occupational status, good education, and good access to health care. This is the dimension in which the South shows up so poorly and which picks out the relatively wealthy industrial states at the other end of the scale. The level of social well-being on this dimension represents poverty and affluence in the broadest sense and must be largely attributed to income. The other dimension has to do with social disorganization and the incidence of social pathologies. This identifies the states with large cities, especially those with substantial deprived minority populations, and also some of the most rapidly growing states where some aspects of social disorganization are related to population instability rather than to poverty.

The independence of these two dimensions is highlighted by the contrasting performance of specific states. Scores on the two indicators from the components analysis show New York at the top on General Socio-economic Well-being, reflecting affluence, and at the bottom on the Social Pathology dimension which picks out the social degradation of New York City. Similarly Massachusetts, with the city of Boston, drops from third to thirty-fifth, California from fourth to forty-seventh, New Jersey from fifth to fortieth, and so on. Conversely the predominantly agricultural states of the plains, such as the Dakotas and Iowa, perform much less well on the affluence-related dimension than on social disorganization. To achieve a good overall or aggregate performance a state needs a prosperous agricultural economy, and urban areas without ghettos and barrios or which are predominantly middle-class dormitories. The combination of rural poverty and inner-city social problems ensures a state a position near the bottom of the scale.

An inportant point which might be explored further is the geographical relationship between social well-being and population trends. On both the Social Pathology and the Mental Health indicators poor performances were registered by Florida, California, and some other southwestern states, i.e., those which have been the major targets of inter-state population migration in recent years. The 1970 Census shows that it is in these states that the highest proportions of people moved there homes in the previous five years. Vance Packard (1972) has recently suggested that the transient existence of the more mobile elements in the population predisposes them to both physical and mental illness, and fosters hedonism and other "nomadic values." The analysis in this chapter appears to support an association between population instability and certain social problems, at the state level. Those who seek to achieve or end their "American dream" in the Florida or southern California sun may thus pay a price, in the form of greater exposure to the pathological behavior associated with living rather anonymous lives without the security of local family ties and community roots.

REFERENCES CITED

Packard, V. (1972), *A Nation of Strangers,* David McKay, New York.

Smith, D. M. (1972), "Towards a Geography of Social Well-being: Inter-state Variations in the United States," in R. Peet, ed., *Geographical Perspectives on American Poverty,* Antipode Monographs in Social Geography, No. 1, Worcester, Mass., pp. 17-46.

Wilson, J. O. (1969), *Quality of Life in the United States: An Excursion into the New Frontier of Socio-Economic Indicators,* Midwest Research Institute, Kansas City, Mo.

CHAPTER 8

INTER-CITY ANALYSES

The analysis of state data can do no more than provide a skeletal description of the geography of American social well-being. To add some flesh to this structure, it is necessary to examine smaller territorial units. Although the time will come when counties or groups of counties can be used for this purpose, it is more practicable at the moment to work at the inter-city level. There is already much interest in the idea of urban indicators, as was pointed out in Chapter 6, and the classification of cities is a well-established geographical pursuit. As a distinct human settlement the individual city or metropolis is obviously a more useful unit of observation than is the state though internal heterogeneity must not be overlooked.

This chapter describes three different studies of American cities. These reveal conceptual variations on the social well-being theme and illustrate alternative approaches to the development of urban indicators as well as providing further substantive information on the geography of social well-being in the United States.

The "Quality of Life" in Eighteen Metropolitan Areas

The first analysis presented is useful for illustrative purposes because it involves a limited number of cities and variables. It is based on a comparative study of what the authors describe as "the quality of life" in Washington, D.C. (Jones and Flax, 1970) and was prepared at the Urban Institute.

The purpose of the original study was threefold: (1) to determine whether living conditions in Washington, D.C., are better or worse than they used to be; (2) to see how conditions in the Washington area compare with those in the seventeen other largest metropolitan areas;

104

(3) to see whether conditions in Washington are improving or deteriorating faster than in the other metropolitan areas. The discussion here is concerned with all eighteen cities rather than focusing on Washington, D.C., and includes some additional manipulations of the data compiled by Jones and Flax.

The authors selected fourteen "quality areas," and identified variables to measure them (see Table 8.1). The ground rules governing this selection were that a wide cross-section of quality considerations should be included, that there should be a consensus as to their importance, that only one "indicator" or variable be used for each quality area, that data should be available for two recent years for comparative purposes, and that the variables should be output-oriented measures of urban quality. A number of major caveats were required concerning the selection of data and its treatment, and the reader should refer to the original report for these (Jones and Flax, 1970, 7-8, 36-63).

Comparable data could not be found on some variables for all the metropolitan areas; the analysis which follows is confined to ten of them. Two methods of developing composite indicators of the present state of the cities will be illustrated, the results compared, and then an indicator of change will be generated.

The first method is an application of the *Standard Score Additive Model* introduced in the previous chapter. Data for each of the ten variables were transformed into Z-scores and these were summed, with the results shown in Table 8.2. All but the first variable (per capita income)

Table 8.1. "Quality of Life" areas and selected indicators, as used by Jones and Flax

Quality Areas	Indicators Used
Income	Per capita money income adjusted for cost-of-living differences.
Unemployment	Percent of labor force unemployed.
Poverty	Percent households with less than $3,000 income.
Housing	Cost of housing a moderate income family of four.
Education	Selective service mental test rejection rate.
Health	Infant (i.e. under one year) deaths per 1,000 live births.
Mental Health	Suicides per 100,000 population.
Air Pollution	A composite index of pollutants.
Public Order	Reported robberies per 100,000 population.
Traffic Safety	Deaths from auto accidents per 100,000 population.
Racial Equality	Ratio between non-white and white unemployment rates.
Community Concern	Per capita contributions to United Fund appeal.
Citizen Participation	Percent of voting-age population that voted in recent Presidential elections.
Social Disintegration	Known narcotics addicts per 10,000 population.

Source: Jones and Flax (1970, 6).

were read as negative (high values were "bad") so the signs for their Z-scores were reversed to produce a summation in which high positive

Table 8.2. Standard scores for eighteen metropolitan areas, on ten "Quality of Life" indicators

City or Metropolitan Area	Adjusted per capita Income 1967	Unemployment Rate (%) 1968	Low Income Households (%) 1968	Housing Cost/year ($) (family of four) 1968	Service Mental Test Rejections (%) 1968	Infant Mortality (per 1000 live births) 1967	Suicides (per million population) 1967	Air Pollution Index 1966	Robbery Rate (per 100,000 pop.) 1968	Traffic Deaths (per million pop.) 1967	Sum of Z-scores	Ranking on ΣZ
New York	0.86	0.44	−0.21	−1.36	−1.27	−0.56	0.72	−1.59	−1.85	1.68	−3.14	16
Los Angeles	1.49	−1.83	−0.99	0.33	0.23	1.03	−2.51	−0.74	−0.31	−1.49	−5.29	18
Chicago	1.43	0.44	0.81	−0.94	−0.97	−1.52	0.51	−1.12	−0.54	0.61	−1.33	12
Philadelphia	−0.72	0.17	−0.07	0.54	−0.97	−1.75	0.29	−0.88	0.84	0.41	−2.13	13
Detroit	0.87	−0.63	1.38	0.60	−0.07	−0.56	0.04	−0.43	−1.07	−0.36	−0.26	10
Boston	−1.08	1.10	1.55	−1.75	0.23	1.31	0.74	−0.68	0.97	1.05	3.45	3
San Francisco	1.66	−1.96	−1.34	−0.80	0.54	1.37	−2.75	1.12	−1.07	−1.55	−4.79	17
Washington, D.C.	−0.03	0.84	1.52	−0.15	−2.18	0.58	0.53	0.13	−1.08	0.55	0.70	6
Pittsburgh	−0.81	−1.43	−0.39	1.26	0.84	0.18	0.42	−0.69	0.59	0.11	0.06	9
St. Louis	−0.77	0.30	−0.67	0.19	0.54	−1.29	0.08	−0.42	0.08	−1.13	−3.09	15
Cleveland	−0.01	−0.23	0.46	−1.05	−0.07	0.41	0.04	−0.70	0.32	0.96	0.13	8
Baltimore	−0.38	−0.10	0.07	1.17	−0.67	−0.78	0.53	−0.23	−1.64	−0.19	−2.23	14
Houston	−0.65	0.04	−1.45	1.66	−0.67	−0.05	−0.11	1.38	−0.01	−0.66	−0.53	11
Minneapolis	0.55	1.24	0.63	−0.10	1.74	1.20	0.14	1.07	0.46	−0.31	6.64	1
Dallas	0.32	1.37	−1.20	1.36	−0.07	−0.84	0.17	2.11	1.05	−1.63	2.64	5
Cincinnati	−0.75	0.57	−1.10	0.36	0.23	0.69	0.10	0.16	1.13	1.27	2.67	4
Milwaukee	0.03	0.57	0.95	−0.82	1.44	0.92	0.12	0.48	1.23	0.63	5.55	2
Buffalo	−2.01	−0.90	0.07	−0.50	1.14	−0.33	0.95	1.03	0.90	0.05	0.40	7

Sources of data: Jones and Flax (1970).

figures would be "good" and high negative figures "bad." The eighteen cities have been ranked on this composite indicator. The three with the highest quality of life by this method are Minneapolis, Milwaukee, and Boston. Those with lowest quality of life are Los Angeles, San Francisco, and New York.

An examination of the individual Z-scores reveals the conditions which are particularly influential in determining a city's general quality of life. Among the three best cities, Minneapolis performs especially well (i.e., one standard deviation above the mean) on employment and mental test, Milwaukee on the mental test, and Boston on unemployment, low income households, infant mortality, and traffice deaths (more than compensating for poor performance on per capita income and housing cost). The worst three cities show Los Angeles doing badly (Z-scores of more than one standard deviation below the mean) on unemployment, suicide, and traffic deaths, though per capita income is high; San Francisco does badly on unemployment, low income households, suicide, robbery, and traffic deaths, but scores well on per capita income, infant mortality, and air pollution; New York has poor scores on housing cost, mental test, air pollution, and robbery, but the best score of all the cities on traffic deaths. The Z-scores thus provide a quality-of-life profile for each city, as well as permitting the generation of a composite indicator.

The second method of developing a general indicator is through a *Ranking Additive Model*. This simply involves the ranking of the metropolitan areas on each variable, giving rank 1 to the lowest value for all but per capita income (where top rank goes to the highest), and then summing ranks for each place, i.e.,

$$S_j = \sum_{i=1}^{m} R_{ij} \ ,$$

where S_j is the level of social well-being or life quality in city j, and
R_{ij} is the ranking of city j on variable i,
and the summation is over m variables, in this case ten.

Finally, the cities are re-ranked on the composite score, with rank 1 for the "best" city and 18 for the "worst." A comparison (not reproduced here) with the rankings on the composite indicator from the Standard Score Model shows little difference between the two. Spearman's rank correlation coefficient is 0.919. Thus the two different models order the cities in a very similar manner.

Table 8.3. Rankings for change for eighteen metropolitan areas, on ten "Quality of Life" indicators

City or Metropolitan Area	Adjusted per capita Income 1966-67	Unemployment Rate 1967-68	Low Income Households 1967-68	Housing Costs 1967-68	Service Mental Test Rejections 1967-68	Infant Mortality 1966-67	Suicide Rate 1966-67	Robbery Rate 1967-68	Traffic Deaths 1966-67	Voting in Presidential Election 1964-68	Sum of Ranks	Final Ranking
New York	5.5	2	5	5	6	11	3.5	17	11	17	83	4
Los Angeles	10.5	3	15.5	11	8	7	11.5	6	7	16	95.5	12
Chicago	10.5	8	4	1	10	4.5	5	2	5.5	12	62.5	1
Philadelphia	10.5	5	7.5	8.5	16	17.5	9	13	18	9.5	114.5	15
Detroit	18	4	7.5	12	18	12.5	11.5	4	3	7	91.5	8
Boston	2	6	2	8.5	7	9	11.5	15	4	7	72.5	3
San Francisco	14	7	15.5	18	14.5	7	8	18	13	12	127	18
Washington, D.C.	16.5	18	7.5	10	11	1	2	14	15	3	98	13
Pittsburgh	5.5	10	12	6	17	14.5	11.5	16	14	4.5	111	14
Stl Louis	14	1	12	4	4.5	12.5	14	12	8.5	12	94.5	10
Cleveland	16.5	12	12	15	12	14.5	7	1	12	14.5	116.5	16
Baltimore	10.5	10	18	2	9	7	1	11	17	9.5	95	11
Houston	5.5	15	7.5	14	14.5	2	17	7	10	1	93.5	9
Minneapolis	1	17	12	3	2	16	3.5	9	2	4.5	69	2
Dallas	5.5	10	2	13	13	10	18	3	8.5	2	85	5.5
Cincinnati	5.5	16	17	7	4.5	3	16	8	1	7	85	5.5
Milwaukee	5.5	14	2	16.5	1	4.5	6	5	16	18	88	7
Buffalo	14	13	12	16.5	3	17.5	15	10	5.5	14.5	121	17

Source: Jones and Flax (1970).

A major objective of the development of social indicators is to monitor change over time. Jones and Flax (1970) attempted this for their eighteen metropolitan areas. They obtained data for two different years for ten of their variables—those used in the analysis above except that presidential election voting replaces air pollution. Then the cities were ranked on each variable according to the magnitude of change, with the largest change in the desirable direction given rank 1. As the authors pointed out, a one-year time span is too short a period to detect significant trends, but this exercise was purely for illustrative purposes. The ranks are listed in Table 8.3.

In an attempt to develop a general city indicator of change in the quality of life, the ranks from the Jones and Flax study have been summed (Table 8.3). The smaller sum, the better the city has performed. A re-ranking of these data shows Chicago as the most improved city, with Minneapolis second and Boston third. The least improved cities are San Francisco, Buffalo, and Cleveland. A correlation with the ranks on existing quality of life produced a coefficient of .391. Thus, in general, the better the rank of the city the better its rank on change, though the correlation is not high enough to be significant at the 95% confidence level.

This analysis is merely suggestive of what might be achieved, given better time-series data. With accurate measures of change in a wide range of conditions which relate to social well-being, over an adequate period of years, some general indicators of social change could be developed. These could show whether the cities are really getting better or worse, and at what rate, and help to identify the conditions which have the greatest bearing on these trends.

Goal Attainment Levels in Metropolitan Areas

The study described above has done no more than introduce the development of city social indicators. If some observations are to be made on geographical variations in the state of American cities, against some broad concept of social well-being, a larger number of places must be examined and more variables must be used. The most ambitious study at this scale to date is an attempt by Coughlin (1970) to identify "goal attainment levels" for the 101 largest Standard Metropolitan Statistical Areas.

Sixty individual "goal attainment indicators" were selected. They were chosen by "general knowledge of the literature in metropolitan and urban planning, government, and sociology, economics, etc., rather than direct survey or a systematic analytical procedure" (Coughlin, 1970, 5); in other words, in a similar manner to that used in the state analysis in Chapter 7. They are measures of results (i.e., output) rather than of effort, and the goal attainment level is related in some way to public policy. No priority weightings are assigned. Each goal attainment indicator is defined in such a way that a higher numerical value is always more desirable than a lower level and the higher the value the better. The desirability of increasing the achievement level of each goal stands by itself and is not contingent upon change in some other condition. The analysis is concerned with the level of goal achievement at one particular time and does not measure change. Finally, the choice of variables was restricted by data availability.

The indicators are listed in Table 8.4, grouped under seventeen general categories. It was found much easier to measure social and economic characteristics than physical conditions relating to environmental quality despite the attention which city planners often give to goals such as the reduction of traffic congestion and water pollution. Nevertheless, Coughlin's list covers a very broad range of conditions which impinge on the quality of human existence in metropolitan areas.

As a first step in the manipulation of data on these variables, Coughlin transformed them into standard scores. These provide a goal attainment profile for each metropolitan area, showing how it compares with others and with the norm for all large SMSAs. As an example, the Z-scores for the Tampa-St. Petersburg SMSA in Florida are listed in Table 8.4, along with the original data and the SMSA means. A negative Z-score indicates below average goal attainment and a positive score is above average.

The sum of the Z-Scores for each metropolitan area may be treated as a general social indicator in the same way as in previous analyses.* Considerable variations in the overall goal attainment level are revealed, with this general indicator ranging in magnitude from 40.4 in Rochester, New York, down to—46.9 in Mobile, Alabama.

Mapping these scores provides a general picture of geographical variations in metropolitan goal attainment (Figure 8.1). A very clear pattern

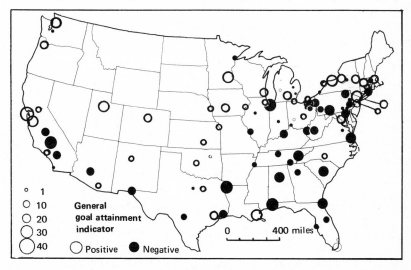

Figure 8.1 The geographical pattern of metropolitan goal attainment, based on a summation of standard scores on Coughlin's sixty indicators. (Source: data by courtesy of Dr. R. E. Coughlin, Regional Science Research Institute.)

*The author is grateful to Dr. R. E. Coughlin, Research Associate at the Regional Science Research Institute, for making his original data available for this analysis.

Table 8.4. Metropolitan goal attainment indicators as used by Coughlin, with sample data

Criteria and Goal Indicators	SMSA mean	Tampa–St. Petersburgh SMSA value	Z-score
Purity of Air			
1 Air free of particulate matter—minimum concentration	789	874	1,2
2 Air free of particulate matter —geometric mean	884	914	0.9
3 Air free of organic matter—minimum concentration	80.2	86.7	0.8
4 Air free of organic matter—geometric mean	91.2	93.5	0.8
Open Space			
5 Public open space utility index	18.4	7.5	−0.3
Health			
6 Infant survival rate	75.0	71.9	−0.9
7 Age normalized general survival rate	91.3	92.6	0.6
Political and Governmental Well-being			
8 Population per local government unit	12,726	19,311	0.4
9 Percent electorate voting in gubernatorial election	53.1	48.4	−0.3
10 Balance of political power	83.9	70.9	−1.0
Education			
11 Median school years completed by persons 25 and over	11.0	10.6	−0.5
12 Percent population 25 and over completed 5 or more years school	93.0	92.8	−0.1
13 Percent population 25 and over completed high school or more	43.9	40.5	−0.5
14 Percent population 25 and over completed college or more	7.1	6.0	−0.6
15 Percent population 14-17 in school	88.1	86.0	−0.6
Housing			
16 Percent dwelling units sound, with all plumbing	79.9	82.5	0.4
17 Percent dwelling units uncrowded	89.2	90.0	0.3
18 Percent dwelling units owner occupied	63.4	73.7	1.3
19 Rental occupancy score	90.8	82.0	−0.8
Income and Wealth			
20 Median income of families	6,077	4,490	−2.2
21 Percent families with incomes $3000 or over per year	83.6	70.0	−2.4
22 Bank deposits per capita	1.4	1.0	−0.6
Economic Equality			
23 Median income of males over 14, negro/white	0.6	0.7	0.6
24 Unemployment rate for males 14 and over, white/non-white	0.5	0.8	1.6
Housing Integration			
25 Block index of residential integration	13.6	5.5	−1.3
26 Center city-suburban ring integration index	66.6	81.8	0.9
Employment Rate			
27 Percent persons in labor force employed	94.9	94.9	0.0
Normal Family Structure			
28 Percent married women with husband & children not in labor force	80.6	76.4	−1.1
29 Percent families with children, father and mother	91.2	89.2	−1.0
Safety			
30 Index of persons not murdered	94.9	93.9	−0.3
31 Index of females over 18 not raped	92.0	91.9	−0.1
32 Index of persons not killed in motor accidents	80.5	76.1	−0.8

Table 8.4 (cont.)

33 Index of persons not killed in other accidents	71.3	71.0	−0.0
34 Fire safety index	8,514	8,129	−1.1
Availability of Services			
35 College professors etc. per 1000 population	1.0	0.4	−0.8
36 Professionals etc. per 1000 population	43.8	31.9	−1.4
37 Workers in the arts per 1000 population	2.1	1.9	−0.3
38 Physicians per 1000 population	1.4	1.1	−0.9
39 Hotel workers etc. per 1000 population	3.2	4.7	0.7
40 Personal service workers per 1000 population	6.3	7.8	0.4
41 Business service workers per 1000 population	5.3	4.5	−0.3
42 Business repair service workers per 1000 population	1.1	1.3	0.3
43 Amusement etc. workers per 1000 population	1.8	2.1	0.2
44 Eating and drinking place workers per 1000 population	10.7	11.6	0.3
Availability of Transit			
45 Percent workers using public transit	12.3	6.9	−0.7
46 Excess transit use/automobile ownership	0.0	−8.4	−1.7
47 Transit use × automobile availability	997.2	529.7	−0.7
Dominance of Central Core			
58 Percent metropolitan retail sales in CBD	14.5	14.1	−0.1
Lack of Stress and Environment−Related Disease			
49 Suicide deaths: expected/actual	1.0	0.7	−0.9
50 Bronchitis deaths: expected/actual	1.1	1.4	0.5
51 Heart disease deaths: expected/actual	1.1	1.8	1.9
52 Other hypersensitive heart deaths: expected/actual	1.1	1.3	0.4
53 Ulcer deaths: expected/actual	1.0	1.2	0.5
54 Cirrhosis of liver deaths: expected/actual	1.1	1.2	0.2
55 Tuberculosis deaths: expected/actual	1.2	1.8	1.0
56 Malignant neoplasm deaths: expected/actual	1.0	1.0	0.1
57 Asthma deaths: expected/actual	1.1	1.5	0.5
Structural Soundness of Economy			
58 Diversification index	0.0	75.0	0.7
59 Percent employment in growth industries	35.0	45.9	1.7
60 Percent employment in high income industries	22.1	18.5	−0.5

Source: Coughlin (1970, 6-10); data from Dr. Coughlin.

emerges, with low levels in the South and much of the major manufacturing belt, changing to positive values to the North and West except for some large negative scores in the Southwest. The map accurately reflects the broad regional differentiation identified in the inter-state analysis of the previous chapter.

But as at the state level general performance will mask performance in individual criteria of social well-being or goal attainment. Some of these may operate independently, some will appear to conflict, and others will be closely inter-related. Coughlin used factor analysis to identify the underlying patterns of variation; the results give further definition to the basic geography shown in Figure 8.1.

The two leading factors are easily interpretable. The first factor groups together high achievement in basic schooling, high income levels and lack of low incomes, high voting rates and party political balance, income equality and housing integration of central city blacks, families with both parents and mother at home, good balance in housing supply and demand, and low rates of murder and automobile accident deaths. Combined with these features is a relatively low level of certain services, above-average death from ulcers, and a CBD which fails to dominate the metropolis (i.e., dispersed retailing). Coughlin called this factor the *"Middle America" Goal Axis*. Metropolitan areas with the largest positive factor scores are Rochester, Patterson-Clifton-Passiac, Seattle, and New Haven, and they are in general highly concentrated in the eastern part of the major manufacturing belt. SMSAs with large negative scores include Shreveport, Columbia, Norfolk-Portsmouth, and Memphis, and all are concentrated in the South. Coughlin (1970, 38) suggests that the economic, social, and political history of southern metropolitan areas in general has prevented them from achieving high levels of traditional "Middle American" goals.

The second factor groups together high educational achievement, high median income, high employment rate, and sound housing. It also has a variety of services, as represented by high proportions in certain professions and high employment in business and personal services. Coughlin labels this the *Cosmopolitan and Affluence Goal Axis*. Metropolitan areas with the highest positive scores (after Washington, D.C.) are San Jose, San Francisco-Oakland, and Los Angeles in California. The highest negative scores include both southern SMSAs and northern blue-collar industrial centers such as Gary-Hammond, Johnstown, Wilkes-Barre, Reading, and Lancaster.

Four other factors were identified but these are not discussed here (for highest and lowest SMSA scores, see Coughlin, 1970, 34-37).

No real attempt was made to explain differences in metropolitan goal attainment levels. However, the importance of income is clear from the intercorrelation between the original indicators. There are significant positive correlations between at least one of the income variables and at least one indicator in all but four of the seventeen goal categories. The exceptions are Purity of Air, Open Space, Employment Rate, and Dominance of Central Core, three of which relate to "physical" goals. Thus Coughlin (1970, 23) suggests that "if one were to be limited to the specification of a small number of goals, one could subsume many goals under income, and detail a relatively larger set of the physical goals unrelated to income." Income indicators, specifically median income and families with over $3000 a year, are the best single measures of overall goal attainment (Coughlin, 1970, 27).

Social Well-being in Metropolitan Areas

A further metropolitan analysis may be described briefly. It differs from Coughlin's in that the selection of conditions to be included is guided specifically by the concept of social well-being developed in Chapter 6. It is based on 109 SMSAs with populations of 250,000 or more.

This study is offered as an illustration of what may be learned about the inter-city geography of social well-being from the most easily accessible data. The variables included are confined to those for which data are available in the *Metropolitan Area Statistics* section of the *Statistical*

Abstract of the United States. This necessarily means that the general concept of social well-being is not reflected as closely as it was in the inter-state analysis in Chapter 7, and there are some important omissions. Particularly serious is the inability to include a range of variables relating to social disorganization, alienation, and participation. However, this is a preliminary analysis only and one objective of future research should be to develop a more satisfactory operational definition of social well-being suitable for the inter-city level of analysis.

Thirty-one variables have been selected (Table 8.5) under five headings. Material Living Standards includes variables relating to income, wealth, and employment, but with more emphasis on monetary aspects than in the inter-state analysis and less on employment as it affects status. A Welfare Services category is included to cover the various income supplement payments. Health is represented in a more restricted way than in the inter-state analysis and by less direct measures than some of those available by states. The same is true of the Education category, where there are no measures of outputs or educational performance. Social Order is represented by seven categories of crime.

The procedures used here are similar to those in the previous section. The data were transformed into standard scores and these were summed to provide a first general social indicator. When these scores are mapped (Figure 8.2) the pattern is similar to that shown by Coughlin's data (Figure 8.1). However, the regional differentiation is even clearer now, with a very sharp distinction between the belt of negative scores in the South and the positive scores in the Northeast and the northern part of the major manufacturing belt. The southern part of the manufacturing belt appears as a zone of transition. The West, on balance, looks better

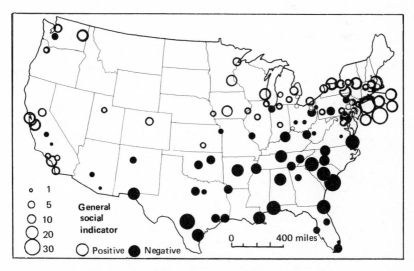

Figure 8.2 The geographical pattern of metropolitan social well-being, based on a summation of standard scores on the 31 variables. (Source of data: see Table 8.5.)

than in Coughlin's data. Few cities perform in a markedly different manner on the two maps; those that do can be explained by extreme scores on some condition included in Coughlin's study but not included in the present one. Thus the concepts of "goal attainment" and "social well-being," as made operational in these two studies portray substantially the same geographical picture.

Table 8.5. *Variables used to measure social well-being in SMSAs with 250,000 or more population*

Criteria and Variables	Direction
Material Living Standards	
1 Annual income per capita ($) 1966	+
2 Annual incomes under $3,000 (%) 1967	–
3 Annual incomes over $20,000 (%) 1967	+
4 Unemployment (% of total workforce) 1968	–
5 Average weekly earnings of production workers ($) 1968	+
6 Local property tax per capita ($) 1967	+
7 Median property value of FHA insured homes ($) 1967	+
8 Total bank deposits per capita ($) 1968	+
9 Total retail sales per capita 1963	+
10 Increase in retail sales (%) 1958-1963	+
Welfare	
11 Local welfare expenditures per capita ($) 1967	+
12 Social Security recipients per 100,000 population 1968	+
13 Total social security payments per recipient ($) Dec. 1968	+
14 Average benefit for retired workers ($) Dec. 1968	+
15 Total anti-poverty funds per capita ($) 1968	+
16 Old age assistance per recipient ($) Feb. 1969	+
17 Families with dependent children assistance per family ($) Feb. 1969	+
Health	
18 Physicians per 100,000 population 1967	+
19 Hospital beds per 100,000 population 1967	+
20 Dentists per 100,000 population 1967	+
21 Local health and hospital expenditures per capita ($) 1967	+
Education	
22 Median school years completed 1960	+
23 Pupils per teacher in public schools 1967-1968	–
24 Local education expenditures per capita ($) 1967	+
Social Order or Disorganization (Crime)	
25 Murder and manslaughter per 100,000 population 1968	–
26 Forcible rape per 100,000 population 1968	–
27 Robbery per 100,000 population 1968	–
28 Aggravated assault per 100,000 population 1968	–
29 Burglary per 100,000 population 1968	–
30 Larceny $50 and over per 100,000 population 1968	–
31 Auto theft per 100,000 population 1968	–

Source of data: U.S. Bureau of the Census, *Metropolitan Area Statistics*, reprinted from *Statistical Abstract of the United States*, 1969, USGPO, Washington, D.C.

A principle components analysis has been used to expose the major dimensions of variance in the data. The first component accounts for almost thirty percent of the original variance (Table 8.6), and its emphasis

Table 8.6. Structure of the two leading components of social well-being among SMSAs with over 250,000 population

COMPONENT 1: *AFFLUENCE* (explained variance: 27.9%)
highest loadings: .8466 per capita property tax
.8350 per capita income
.7657 aid to dependent children payments
.7268 per capital retail sales
.7253 dentists per capita
.7237 social security payments
.6990 incomes of over $20,000
.6580 benefits for retired
.6424 local education expenditures
.6328 per capita bank deposits
.6197 value of homes

COMPONENT 2: *CRIME* (explained variance: 16.5%)
highest loadings: .8140 burglary
.7922 rape
.7564 assault
.7500 murder
.6821 larceny
.6537 robbery
−.4854 benefits for retired
−.4812 social security payments
−.4724 aid to dependent children payments
.4547 auto theft

Note: From the principal axis solution, without rotation.

on income and wealth leads to the indentification of *Affluence.* Its composition is similar to that of the General Socio-economic Well-being component of the inter-state analysis (Chapter 7), and it bears some resemblance to Coughlin's Cosmopolitan and Affluence Goal Axis. The second component is clearly *Crime,* associated with some low income-supplement payments. The two leading components together account for forty-four percent of the original variance; the geographical analysis which follows is confined to them.

The SMSA scores on these components may be regarded as general metropolitan indicators representing two independent dimensions of social well-being. Scores on the Affluence component clearly reveal the relative poverty in the South, and the comparative advantage of many cities in the West, the Plains, the Midwest and the Northeast. Poor performance on the Crime component is a characteristic of some south-western cities as well as many in the old South, while the best perfor-mances are in the North and in particular in some of the smaller industrial cities of the manufacturing belt. Maps of these two sets of scores will be found in Smith (1972).

Further insight into the geography of social well-being at the inter-city level is gained when individual city performance on the two leading components is compared. In Figure 8.3 the two sets of scores are plotted

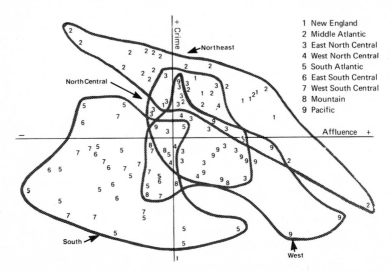

Figure 8.3 Graph of metropolitan area scores on the two leading components of social well-being, with SMSA identified by census region and major division.

and SMSAs identified by Census regions and major divisions of the country. The graph shows a distinct tendency for cities in the same part of the country to occupy a similar position, i.e., they have a similar performance on the two components of social well-being. The line bounding the cities of the South shows little overlap with other regions; most cities have negative scores on both Affluence and Crime, which accounts for their poor position on the general indicator mapped in Figure 8.2. North Central cities generally have positive scores on Affluence but many have negative scores on Crime. The cities of the West occupy a similar position to those of the North Central region on Affluence, but tend to be worse on Crime.

The position of the SMSA of the Northeast is of special interest. Whereas scores on the Affluence and Crime components are uncorrelated nationally (in itself an observation worth noting), this is not necessarily true at the regional level. In the Northeast there is in fact a relationship quite close to linear, but in a negative direction (low incidence of crime associated with low affluence). At the one end of the group are a number of Pennsylvania industrial cities, including Johnstown, Wilkes-Barre - Hazelton, Lancaster, Allentown, Bethlehem-Easton, and Reading, populated by law-abiding blue-collar workers with relatively low levels of affluence. Towards the other end are the more heterogeneous larger cities with higher average affluence but with greater aggregate poverty and a larger criminal community. The distinction appears to be between the "lower class" or "working class" of the smaller industrial cities, and the "underclass" in the socially-deprived environment of the inner-city slums. It should also be noted that property crimes and auto-theft can rise with affluence, simply because there is more to steal.

As in the state analysis reported in Chapter 7, it seems premature to attempt to test specific explanatory hypotheses. However, the results of some correlations may at least suggest some of the causal factors operating on SMSA levels of social well-being. Table 8.7 lists correlation coefficients

Table 8.7. *Correlation (r) between metropolitan social indicators and other selected variables*

Variable	Affluence Indicator	Crime Indicator
1. Distance, west-east	$-.16$	.32
2. Distance, south-north	.50	.57
3. Total population 1967	.54	$-.28$
4. Population per square mile 1966	.34	$-.01$
5. Population change (%) 1960-66	.15	$-.46$
6. Net population migration (% total) 1960-66	.23	$-.36$
7. Non-white population (%) 1960	$-.37$	$-.61$
8. Employment in manufacturing (%) 1968	.05	.57
9. Change in manufacturing employment (%) 1958-63	.07	$-.26$

Note: The indicators are component scores.

between scores on the Affluence and Crime components and other selected conditions. The two distance variables show results similar to the state analysis (see Table 7.4), with south-north coordinate location a better predictor than west-east position. The best single predictor of the level of affluence is the city size measured by population; the bigger the city the better the performance on this indicator. On the Crime indicator the non-white population and population change are fairly good negative predictors (i.e., poor performance is associated with population growth and large proportions of non-whites), while high manufacturing employment is associated with low crime.

A stepwise multiple regression analysis of variables 3-9 on the Affluence and Crime component scores revealed relationships in which more than half the variance could be accounted for by three independent variables. On Affluence, the correlation with population size, non-white population, and migration produced the result $R = .717$ and $R^2 = .514$; the addition of manufacturing growth and population density raised it to $R = .745$ and $R^2 = .555$; on Crime, non-white population, manufacturing employment, and population change, gave $R = .777$ and $R^2 = .604$; the addition of population size and migration raised it to $R = .827$ and $R^2 = .685$. Thus at the SMSA level affluence is associated with a large population having a small proportion of non-whites and relatively rapid migrational increase. Good performance in the Crime indicator is associated with a small proportion of non-whites, a high proportion employed in manufacturing (i.e., blue-collar workers), and population stability.

The Inter-city Geography of Social Well-being

Some tentative conclusions may now be offered concerning geographical variation in social well-being between cities, and the possible causal mechanisms involved.

By most individual criteria, as well as by the general indicators developed in this chapter, social well-being in American cities generally improves away from the South. Western cities perform well on criteria related to affluence, but poorly on social pathology. Most of the midwestern and northern cities perform relatively well on most criteria though there are some exceptions such as the low affluence levels in certain industrial cities and the high though localized incidence of crime and other social pathologies in the major metropolitan areas.

The consistently poor performance of the mass of cities in the South appears to be the salient overall feature of the geography of metropolitan social well-being. This does much to account for the existence of the Southern Region of Social Deprivation. But, as at the state level, the use of variables related to income without allowance for the lower cost of living will unduly depress the scores of southern cities on some indicators. This explains relatively little of the poor performance on many variables, however; for example, cost of living differences account for only about one-sixth of the range in AFDC payments between cities (U.S. Department of Health, Education and Welfare, 1969, 23-24). In fact, it would be extremely difficult to show southern cities in a very much more favorable light, even with a deliberate selection of conditions and a standardization for racial composition as well as for living costs.

Why do southern cities generally perform so badly? To answer this in full would clearly require a detailed examination of the history, culture, and values of the South—an undertaking outside the scope of this book. But on the face of it, this arises in large part from relatively poor performances in the two leading independent dimensions of social well-being along which American metropolitan areas appear to be differentiated. With respect to general socio-economic status, or affluence, southern cities tend to have relatively large proportions of poor people (generally black) and the health, education, and welfare services tend to be less well developed than in other regions. Part of this may be simply a function of limited resources but it must be attributed also to some extreme manifestations of the not uncommon American belief that the poor are unworthy and possibly more so if they are non-white. The low levels of welfare payments in most southern cities and states is a clear expression of these attitudes. The poor performance of most southern cities on the other major dimensions of social well-being also has some class and racial origins. This dimension is identified with social pathologies such as crime, or with non-fulfillment of "Middle-American" goals (according to Coughlin, 1970) and the poor blacks of the South are disproportionately afflicted by these conditions. On top of this is the predisposition towards violence in the South, noted by criminologists for some time, which itself may be an outcome of the peculiar stresses of a relatively poor region in which the forceful oppression of the black population was until recently an accepted way of life.

By way of contrast, the larger cities of the North perform better because their greater affluence offsets the pathological behavior in the ghetto on any general indicator of social well-being. The smaller industrial metropolitan areas are less affluent but there are also smaller ghettos and less social deviance. The great contrast between the law-abiding "ethnics" in the regular if somewhat unrewarding blue-collar jobs and the pathological behavior of the unemployed or underemployed inner-city blacks has obvious public-policy implications; if more blue-collar jobs in factories and on construction sites were open to blacks their holders might take on a less deviant life style than that adopted in their present deprived social environment.

Western cities tend to show the extremes. The affluence associated with technologically-advanced industry is exemplified in the rapidly-growing Californian metropolitan areas. But this strong performance on the affluence dimension appears to be achieved at the price of greater tensions than in cities in most other parts of the country and higher incidence of physical and mental stress-induced illness. Poor performance on the pathology dimension also reflects the instability of a population with many immigrants, some of whom are chicanos and blacks subject to the usual abuses and deprivation of racial minorities. The perpetuation of something of the hustling, anxiety and violence of the frontier days in this region of ethnic and socio-economic heterogeneity thus produces distinctive cities. With its extremes of conspicuous material affluence and untreated social degradation the urban West may still be considered "wild."

REFERENCES CITED

Coughlin, R. E. (1970), *Goal Attainment Levels in 101 Metropolitan Areas,* Regional Science Research Institute, Discussion Paper No. 41, Philadelphia, Pa.

Jones, M. V. and Flax, M. J. (1970), *The Quality of Life in Metropolitan Washington, D.C.: Some Statistical Benchmarks,* The Urban Institute, Washington, D.C.

Smith, D. M. (1972), "Towards a Geography of Social Well-being: Interstate Variations in the United States," in R. Peet, ed., *Geographical Perspectives on American Poverty,* Antipode Monographs in Social Geography, No. 1, Worcester, Mass., pp. 14-46.

U.S. Department of Health, Education and Welfare (1969), *Welfare Policy and its Consequences for the Recipient Population: A Study of the AFDC Program,* USGPO, Washington, D.C.

CHAPTER 9

AN INTRA-CITY ANALYSIS

At the inter-state and inter-city levels, a major problem in the development and interpretation of territorial social indicators is population heterogeneity within the unit of observation. Conditions measured by averages, and by the relations between averages, can be a fortuitous outcome of the contrasting experiences of quite different groups of people. It is only within the city that this problem can be largely overcome by working with relatively homogeneous sub-areas or communities.

This chapter describes an attempt to develop intra-city indicators. It is performed in the context of a particular practical planning problem—that of identifying the "target areas" for programs aimed at improving the quality of life of deprived urban residents. The study is set in the City of Tampa, Florida.*

Problem Areas in Tampa: Background

Tampa is a city of a little over 300,000 persons, on the western side of the Florida Peninsula. It has a distinctive ethnic composition, with a substan-

*The research reported here was conducted by the author on a contract between the Urban Studies Bureau, University of Florida, and the City Demonstration Agency (now Metropolitan Development Agency), City of Tampa. The results are preliminary and the conclusions tentative. Although the assistance of MDA personnel was involved throughout the project, the views expressed here are the author's alone. The contribution of Robert J. Gray as research assistant is gratefully acknowledged; this chapter incorporates material from his MA thesis (Gray, 1972), and from a report prepared for the City of Tampa (Smith and Gray, 1972). The author also acknowledges a fruitful collaboration with Dr. Joshua C. Dickinson, III, of the Geography Department, University of Florida, who initiated a study of Gainesville, Florida (Dickinson, Gray and Smith, 1972), in which some of the procedures used in the Tampa study were pre-tested.

tial Latin community (about ten percent) as well as almost twenty percent black population. It shares with most other large American cities the characteristic of pockets of poverty and social deprivation in the inner-city contrasting sharply with the more affluent suburban areas.

In the middle of the 1960s the U.S. Department of Commerce, Bureau of the Census (1967) carried out a classification and mapping of "poverty areas" in SMSAs with populations of 250,000 or more. Five poverty-linked socio-economic characteristics used were as follows:

1. Percent of families with cash incomes under $3000.
2. Percent of children under 18 years old not living with both parents.
3. Percent of males 25 years old and over with less than 8 years of school completed.
4. Percent of unskilled males (laborers and service workers) aged 14 and over in the employed civilian labor force.
5. Percent of all housing units lacking some or all plumbing facilities or dilapidated.

Data by tracts from the 1960 Census were used to produce a composite "poverty index," and tracts falling into the lowest quartile were designated "poor." By this method, roughly half of the City of Tampa was defined as a poverty area (see Figure 9.1).

In 1967 Tampa entered the Model Cities program, under the Demonstration Cities and Metropolitan Development Act of 1966. A Model Neighborhood Area (MNA) was identified as the target area for various projects aimed at permanently raising the socio-economic and physical standards of living of the most deprived population groups. The MNA comprised six tracts (as defined for the 1970 Census) and part of three others. It had a total population of almost 35,000, two-thirds of them black. The problems of this area could reasonably be described as severe, with forty-five percent of households at or below the poverty level, one in five dependent on welfare, almost fourteen percent of the labor force unemployed, almost forty percent of all residential structures substandard, an above-average incidence of social pathologies such as juvenile delinquency and venereal disease, and low levels of heath and education. The MNA, identified in Figure 9.1, was thus the city's hard core problem area. It lies mainly in the vicinity of Ybor City, immediately to the northeast of the Tampa CBD.

In mid-1971 Tampa was selected as one of twenty cities to participate in a new program termed Planned Variation. This was, in effect, an expansion of the existing Model Cities program to facilitate implementation of revenue sharing, through which further federal funds were made available to help combat urban problems. One requirement of the new program was that plans should be carried out on a citywide basis and not confined to the existing MNA and this necessitated the redefinition of target areas. A preliminary delimitation was made by the City Demonstration Agency, using the following criteria:

1. Housing conditions.
2. Physical conditions.
3. Health.
4. Crime and delinquency.
5. Unemployment.
6. Welfare services.

Data on twenty-one variables under these headings were used to rank census tracts and this was supplemented by detailed knowledge of local conditions. As a result, Primary Target Areas were identified, comprising twenty-two tracts and part of six others (Figure 9.1).

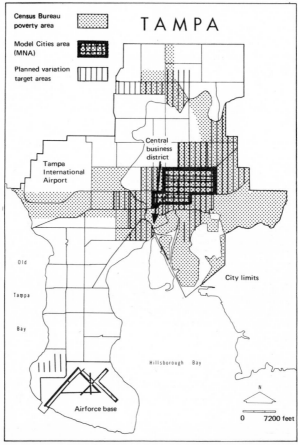

Figure 9.1 Three alternative definitions of "problem areas" in Tampa, Florida. The subdivisions are census tracts. (Source: Smith and Gray, 1972.)

The Selection of Data for Intra-city Indicators

In the fall of 1971 a social indicators research project was initiated in Tampa. The purpose was to extend the data base for problem identification, program design, and project evaluation for the Metropolitan Development Agency which replaced the City Demonstration Agency. One outcome was a check on the identification of problem areas.

The selection of data was guided by the concept of social well-being as developed earlier in this book. The six major criteria used in the inter-state study in Chapter 7 were adopted and data on forty-seven variables were assembled (Table 9.1). Unlike the usual geographical studies of urban social ecology, census variables are in a minority here. It was originally

Table 9.1.   Criteria of social well-being and variables used in Tampa study

Criteria and Variables		
I ECONOMIC STATUS		
i) *Income*		
1 Income per capita ($) of persons 14 and over 1970	+	(1)
2 Families with income less than $3000 (%) 1970	–	(1)
3 Families with income over $10,000 (%) 1970	+	(1)
4 Persons in families below poverty level (%) 1970	–	(1)
ii) *Employment*		
5 Unemployed persons (% total workforce) 1970	–	(1)
6 Persons aged 16-24 working less than 40 weeks (%) 1969	–	(1)
7 White-collar workers (%) 1970	+	(1)
8 Blue-collar workers (%) 1970	–	(1)
iii) *Welfare*		
9 Families on AFDC program (%) October 1971	–	(2)
10 Persons aged 65 and over on Old Age Assistance (%) Oct. 1971	–	(2)
II ENVIRONMENT		
i) *Housing*		
11 Average value of owner-occupied units ($) 1970	+	(1)
12 Owner-occupied units valued less than $10,000 (%) 1970	–	(1)
13 Average monthly rental of rented units ($) 1970	+	(1)
14 Rented units with monthly rentals less than $60 (%) 1970	–	(1)
15 Units with complete plumbing facilities (%) 1970	+	(1)
16 Deteriorating and dilapidated houses (%) 1971	–	(3)
ii) *Streets and Sewers*		
17 Streets needing reconstruction (% of total length) 1971	–	(4)
18 Streets needing scarification and resurfacing (% of total length)1971	–	(4)
19 Sanitary sewer deficiencies (% of total area) 1971	–	(5)
20 Storm sewer deficiencies (% of total area) 1971	–	(4)
iii) *Air Pollution*		
21 Maximum monthly dustfall (tons/sq. mile) 1969	–	(6)
22 Average suspended particulates 1969 (μgm/m^3/day) 1969	–	(6)
23 Maximum monthly sulfation 1969 (mg SO$_3$/100 cm^2/day) 1969	–	(6)
vi) *Open space*		
24 Area lacking park and recreation facilities (%) 1971	–	(7)
III HEALTH		
i) *General Mortality*		
25 Infant deaths (per 1000 live births) 1970	–	(8)
26 Death rate (per 10,000 persons 65 or over) 1970	–	(8)
ii) *Chronic Diseases*		
27 Cancer deaths (per 100,000 population) 1970	–	(8)
28 Stroke deaths (per 100,000 population) 1970	–	(8)
29 Heart disease deaths (per 100,000 population) 1970	–	(8)
30 New active tuberculosis cases (per 10,000 population) 1970	–	(8)
IV EDUCATION		
i) *Duration*		
31 Persons aged 18-24 with 4 or more years high school or college (%) 1970	+	(1)
i 32 Persons over 25 with 8 years or less school (%) 1970	–	(1)
33 Persons over 25 with 4 years high school (%) 1970	+	(1)
34 Persons over 25 with 4 years college (%) 1970	+	(1)

Table 9.1 (cont.)

V SOCIAL DISORGANIZATION

i) *Personal Pathologies*

35 Narcotic violations arrests (per 10,000 residents) 1971	–	(9)
36 Venereal disease cases (per 10,000 population) 1970	–	(8)

ii) *Family Breakdown*

37 Families with children, having husband and wife present (%) 1970	+	(1)
38 Persons separated or divorced (% ever married) 1970	–	(1)

iii) *Overcrowding*

39 Dwellings with more than 1.0 persons per room (%) 1970	–	(1)

iv) *Public Order and Safety*

40 Criminal violation arrests (per 1000 residents) 1971	–	(9)
41 Juvenile delinquency arrests (per 10,000 residents) 1971	–	(9)
42 Accidental deaths (per 100,000 population) 1970	–	(8)

v) *Delinquency*

43 Juvenile delinquency arrests by residency (per 10,000 population) 1971	–	(9)

VI PARTICIPATION AND EQUALITY

i) *Democratic Participation*

44 Registered voters (% population 18 and over) 1971	+	(10)
45 Eligible voters voting in mayoral election (%) 1971	+	(10)

ii) *Equality*

46 Racial distribution index 1970	–	(1)
47 Income distribution index 1970	–	(1)

Sources of data: (1) *1970 Census of Population and Housing,.* (2) Division of Family Services, State of Florida. (3) Hillsborough County Planning Commission. (4) Department of Public Works, City of Tampa. (5) Sanitary Sewers Department, City of Tampa. (6) Hillsborough County Pollution Control Commission. (7) Metropolitan Development Agency, City of Tampa. (8) Hillsborough County Health Department. (9) Police Department, City of Tampa. (10) Supervisor of Elections, City of Tampa.

intended to incorporate attitudinal data on individual perception of life quality and local problems but the cost of a properly conducted survey stratified by census tracts (the spatial unit of observation selected) proved to be too great for the agency's resources.

The specific variables used require brief explanation. Under Economic Status, income levels and stability of employment predominate, the remaining four variables measuring occupational status and welfare dependency. It was possible to measure Environment more broadly than at the state level, with data on some good surrogates for general physical neighborhood quality as well as on housing. Data on Health are more limited, however, and the variables chosen are confined to death rates. In the absence of standard test achievement scores in an appropriate form, Education variables are confined to census measures of duration. Social Disorganization was defined quite broadly, though the form of the local data on arrests limited the crime variables that could be included. The category termed Participation and Equality includes electoral data and measures of racial segregation and income distribution.

As in any project of this kind the final choice of data is a compromise between the ideal and what is possible given the constraints of time and resources. A great deal of effort is required to go beyond census data, converting local agency records into a suitable form, and in some cases the task was too great. However, the data assembled provide a satisfactory reflection of the general concept of social well-being and embody many important conditions which have a bearing on the quality of individual life.

Social Indicators from Standard Scores

The first attempt to develop social indicators followed the Standard Score Additive Model described in the inter-state analysis (Chapter 7). Data on each variable were transformed into Z-scores, and these were summed for the six criteria of social well-being and for all variables. These sums were themselves standardized, to give six criteria indicators and a general social indicator that could be directly compared.

Figure 9.2 shows the poorest tracts on each of the six criteria. Although certainly not identical, the patterns broadly correspond, with a clear

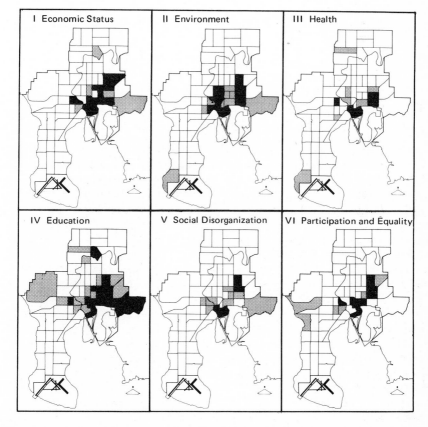

Figure 9.2 The problem areas of Tampa, defined by census tracts with indicator scores of one standard deviation (heavy shading) and a half a standard deviation (light shading) below the mean. (Source of data: see Table 9.1.)

concentration in the sector extending northeast from the CBD across the former Model Cities area (see Figure 9.1). With only three exceptions, all tracts with scores of − 1.0 or worse on any of the six indicators are within the Planned Variation Primary Target Areas (PVPTA). Two of these exceptions are the CBD tracts, which have generally the worst scores of all but which were deliberately excluded from the target areas as special cases. Of the tracts entirely within the PVPTA, only six fail to appear on any of the maps in Figure 9.2. The better tracts (with scores of + 1.0 or more), not shown on these maps, generally occupy the sector to the southwest of the CBD, with some isolated incidences in the north.

The general indicator derived by summing standard scores on all variables is mapped in Figure 9.3. Tampa appears to conform to the sector model of internal spatial structure rather than the concentric zone model, at least insofar as social well-being is concerned. The poor areas extend

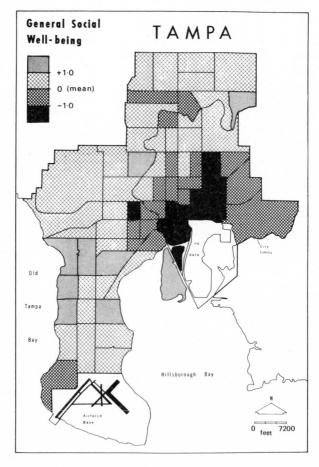

Figure 9.3 Standard scores on a general indicator of social well-being, based on data on all 47 variables listed in Table 9.1. (Source: Smith and Gray, 1972.)

from around the CBD to the city limits in a northeasterly direction while the best areas occupy the opposite sector. Relatively poor tracts appear in isolation in the northern part of the city and in the extreme south.

Like the individual indicators, the general indicator broadly confirms the definition of the PVPTA. There are a few tracts excluded which have worse scores than some within the target areas and these could be incorporated by peripheral expansion. The ordinal position of most tracts changes by a number of places—more than ten in half the tracts. The correlation between the original CDA rankings and those from the composite standard score indicator is .72.

Factors of Intra-city Social Well-being

One of the shortcomings of the standard score summation approach to the development of social indicators is that it fails to reflect underlying dimensions of variance in the data matrix. There may be conflicting patterns of variation within particular criteria: for example, in Tampa the five census housing measures are very weakly related to other environmental quality variables. And there may be similarities between elements of different criteria, as in the fairly close correlation between income, occupational status, education, and value of housing.

In an attempt to reveal something of the structure of interrelationships between social conditions in Tampa, a factor analysis has been run.* The principal-axes solution produced a first factor accounting for thirty-six percent of the original variance, with high loadings on most measures of economic status, housing quality, health, education, and social disorganization. Scores on this factor would clearly provide a good general social indicator as was the case with the leading principal-axes factor or component at the inter-state and inter-city levels. But the objective here is different than that in the other studies, being more concerned with the structure of interrelationships than with efficiency of data compression. Therefore the ten leading factors were subjected to an oblique rotation. This produces new factors which account for less variance individually than their counterparts from the principal-axes solution, but as each variable usually loads high on only one factor the rotated factors can be more easily identified as associated with a specific and limited set of interrelated social conditions. The use of an oblique rotation rather than the common Varimax rotation avoids the imposition of orthogonality on the factor structure, though the Varimax does not differ greatly from the oblique solution in this case.

The development of tract social indicators is based on the four leading oblique factors, which together account for forty-seven percent of the original variance. As they are only weakly correlated with one another they may be interpreted as largely independent dimensions of social well-being. Their identity is suggested by the high-loading variables, as listed in Table 9.2.

*This analysis was conducted by Mr. Robert J. Gray, using the program developed by Guertin and Bailey (1970). The assistance of Dr. W. H. Guertin of the Department of Education, University of Florida, is gratefully acknowledged.

Table 9.2. Highest loadings on leading social well-being factors in Tampa

1. SOCIAL PROBLEMS (explained variance: 17.8%)
    Death rate   .998
    Heart disease deaths   .946
    Cancer deaths   .905
    Criminal violation arrests   .885
    Juvenile delinquency arrests   .851
    Stroke deaths   .789
    Families on AFDC   .682
    Persons separated or divorced   .619
    Juvenile delinquency arrests by residence   .605
    Families with children having husband and wife   .567
    Narcotics violations   .554
    Families with incomes less than $3000   .552
    Venereal disease   .520
    Persons 18-24 with 4 years high school or college   .501

2. SOCIO-ECONOMIC STATUS   (explained variance: 11.3%)
    Persons over 25 with 4 years college   .934
    Average value of owner-occupied housing units   .909
    Income per capita   .744
    Blue-collar workers   .633
    Families with incomes over $10,000   .615
    Maximum monthly sulfation   −.568
    Average monthly rental of rented housing units   .556
    White-collar workers   .548
    Persons over 25 with 8 years school   .533
    Owner-occupied housing units valued less than $10,000   .498
    Registered voters   .454

3. RACIAL SEGREGATION   (explained variance: 9.5%)
    Racial distribution index   .878
    Dwelling with more than 1.0 persons per room   .846
    Persons on Old Age Assistance   .710
    Persons over 25 with 4 years high school   .479
    Persons 18-24 with 4 years high school or college   .465
    Juvenile delinquency arrests by residence   .462
    White-collar workers   .434
    Families on AFDC   .421

4. SOCIAL DEPRIVATION (explained variance: 8.3%)
    Unemployed persons   .834
    New active tuberculosis cases   .810
    Housing units with complete plumbing   .640
    Narcotics violations   .590
    Venereal disease   .513
    Families with children having husband and wife   .450
    Persons in families below poverty level   .441
    Infant deaths   .434

Note: From oblique rotation (primary factor matrix). The loadings are the correlation
coefficients (*r*) between the variables and the factors.

Factor 1 shows high mortality rates associated with high crime and delinquency, families with low incomes and on welfare, broken homes, a high incidence of narcotics violations and venereal disease, and a high proportion of young people who have not finished high school or gone to college. This factor accounts for a little less than one-fifth of the original variance in the forty-seven variables. For convenience, it is given the label *Social Problems*.

Factor 2 shows a clear association between an extended education, relatively expensive housing, high incomes, few blue-collar workers and many white-collar workers, and high proportions registered to vote. These conditions are fairly closely associated with high air pollution by the sulfation measure—the only variable loading relatively high on any of the factors in a direction different from that suggested by the signs in Table 9.1. (This observation is itself significant, for it shows that there is very little conflict between variables within the factors; in other words, a tract with good performance on some variables is rather unlikely to have bad performance on others which load high on the same factor.) This second factor is obviously a reflection of a general social class or affluence/poverty dimension, as conventionally defined by material wealth, education, and occupational status. It is called *Socio-economic Status*.

Factor 3 has its highest loading on the racial distribution index. It is termed *Racial Segregation* and associates overcrowded dwellings, high proportions on the two welfare programs, poor education, and few white-collar workers.

Factor 4 brings together high unemployment, tuberculosis, houses with inadequate plumbing, high narcotics violations and venereal disease, and broken homes. It has some similarity with Factor 1 but appears to identify a set of what might be though of as "hard-core" social problems. It is labeled *Social Deprivation* for want of a better term.

Subsequent factors load high on only a few variables and account for relatively little of the variance in the original data. However, some of them are of interest in identifying small groups of conditions that tend to be quite closely associated with one another but not with most of the remaining variables. For example, Factor 6 includes two of the air pollution variables and the open space index. Factor 9 has its two highest loadings on streets needing reconstruction and storm sewer deficiencies. Factor 10 picks out sanitary sewer deficiencies, streets needing scarification, and deteriorating and dilapidated housing. These observations emphasize that the physical urban environment is not a close reflection of other social problem conditions. This is similar to the conclusion reached by Coughlin (1970) in his inter-city analysis reported in Chapter 8. In the city of Tampa, this may be partly a result of recent neighborhood "face-lift" projects under the Model Cities program, which have had little impact on social problems.

Social Indicators from Factor Analysis

Scores have been calculated for each tract on the four factors described above. These produce territorial social indicators reflecting interrelated sets of conditions, and should thus provide an effective summary of the major features of the geography of social well-being within the City of Tampa. The patterns are illustrated in Figure 9.4.

Factor 1 (Social Problems) shows extremely high negative scores in the two CBD tracts and relatively poor scores in and around the Model Cities area. These are the areas of greatest incidence of the problems identified by the high loadings in Table 9.2. The highest positive scores, indicating

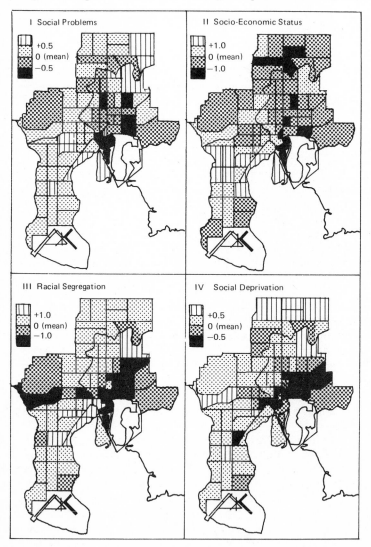

Figure 9.4 Scores on indicators derived from four leading factors of social well-being. The factors are as identified in Table 9.2. (Source: based on maps in Smith and Gray, 1972.)

the lowest incidences, are to the southwest of the city center and in the northeast.

Scores on the Socio-economic Status factor show a clearer concentration of good areas in the southwestern sector, high negative (poor) scores immediately northeast of downtown, and also high negative scores in the northern part of the city included in the Planned Variation Primary Target Areas (see Figure 9.1). High positive scores identify the area of high proportion of affluent, well-housed, well-educated people with high-status jobs, and high negative scores show the reverse.

High negative scores on Factor 3 (Racial Segregation) correspond closely with areas of predominantly black population. These are the tracts with greatest departures from the city average racial composition and with the high incidence of the conditions identified by the high loadings listed in Table 9.2. High positive scores on this indicator generally combine low incidence of these conditions with closer proximity to racial balance.

Scores on Factor 4 (Social Deprivation) provide an indicator of the incidence of certain "hard-core" social problems. High negative scores identify the MNA or the Model Cities area closer than on the other factors. The highest positive scores are mainly in the northern part of the city, including some tracts with relatively poor scores on Socio-economic Status.

There are clearly some similarities between these patterns. Tracts with the poorest performances are largely concentrated in the area to the northeast of the CBD, where the MNA and Planned Variation target areas are situated, as was shown by the standard score indicators in Figures 9.2 and 9.3. The tracts with the best performances are in the southwest and the north. But even within these broad sectors of similarity the relative performance of individual tracts can vary considerably on different indicators. For example, Tract 32 on the western side of the former Model Cities area has a negative score of more than one standard deviation on Socio-economic Status but hovers around the mean on the other indicators, and some of the most affluent southwestern tracts facing Old Tampa Bay do not score much above the mean on Factors 1, 3, and 4.

There are a few more striking contrasts. The area immediately to the south of Tampa International Airport (Tract 46) combines a predominantly black population and a score of -1.45 on Racial Segregation with one of the best performances on Social Deprivation and positive scores on Socio-economic Status and Social Problems. One of the CBD tracts, where almost ninety percent of the population have changed residence since 1965, scores very badly on the social problem factors (1 and 4) but positively on the other two. The northern tracts generally combine relatively low levels on Socio-econmic Status with positive performances on the other factors, particularly Social Deprivation. Like many other cities, Tampa has its black middle-class community, its socially disorganized and highly unstable population around the prosperity symbols of the CBD, and its non-affluent white neighborhoods of generally law-abiding and conforming citizens.

As in the case of the indicators derived from standard scores, those mapped in Figure 9.4 generally support the Planned Variation Primary Target Areas as already defined. This is clearly where the problems are concentrated; only minor alteration would appear justified on the basis of this analysis. However, the indicators do help to highlight the specific nature of the problems and the areas where they are most severe. Looking at the whole city, the incidence of social problems such as crime and delinquency, narcotics, venereal disease, broken homes, high mortality, and so on, as reflected in performance on Factors 1 and 4, is to some degree independent of both socio-economic status and racial composition. Although what is true at the census tract level of population aggregation may not be true of individual human beings, the spatial expression of problem incidence is certainly not simply a reflection of wealth, class, status, and race. And the tendency for physical conditions to vary independently of the major social dimensions fails to support what might be an assumed coincidence of blighted or polluted neighborhoods and severe social problems. However, broad generalizations such as these, based on aggregate data for what are in some cases quite large territories, are subject to refinement on the basis of field observation, survey, and detailed local knowledge at the block and street level.

Some Conclusions

The development of intra-city social indicators, as illustrated by the analysis summarized here, can make a contribution to the formulation and implementation of public urban planning policy. It can assist with the identification of problem areas and with specifying the particular conditions of concern. And the concept of social well-being can provide some structure and discipline to the often almost random collection of data for city planning purposes.

If the interrelationships between variables are still imperfectly understood, some of the empirical associations or apparent independencies can provide pointers to desirable policy changes. For example, the generally weak relationship between physical environmental quality and many social problems calls into question the large allocations of resources to the neighborhood renewal or "face-lift" projects that have been a feature of Model Cities programs. Although visually conspicuous, pleasing to residents, and often politically popular, such schemes do not get to the basic problems. The lack of jobs, low-wage employment, personal immobility, inadequate access to medical care, and the broken homes where criminal or deviant behavior often begins, remain largely untreated social ills, perhaps beyond the control of individual city governments. Increasing the Federal financial contribution through revenue sharing is unlikely to make real impact on these problems without a frontal assault on some of the mechanisms behind the syndromes of social deprivation identified by factor structures and social indicators.

The analysis reported here also has implications for the understanding of urban spatial structure. The factors that emerged depart considerably from those usually found in factorial ecology studies of American cities (see Chapter 4). The predominantly census data used in most of these studies produce a leading factor reflecting social rank or socio-economic status, a second factor related to stage in life cycle, and a third measuring ethnic composition or racial segregation. In the present study Socio-economic and Racial Segregation factors emerge but are sandwiched between two factors measuring social problems or pathologies. The reason for the differences is, of course, the variables included.

A somewhat similar result has been obtained by Downey and Hunt (1972) in Worcester, Massachusetts. They factor analyzed thirty-three "socio-economic and socio-welfare" variables thought to be related to crime, including conditions not measured by census data. Their first factor (orthogonal rotation) was identified as "Social Problems," with high loadings on divorce, alcoholism, mental illness, unemployment, and poverty. It was followed by "Housing" and then by the "Socio-economic" factor. Some breakdown of the usual factorial ecology structures is also evident in the results of a study of social disorganization in Barry, South Wales, by Giggs (1970).

The importance of the conceptualization guiding the selection of variables used was stressed in the discussion of city classification and urban social geography earlier in this book. Existing approaches were questioned on the grounds of undue reliance on census data and the implicit acceptance of the Census Bureau's restricted criteria of relevance. When the largely demographic and economic data from the census are augmented or replaced by information on the broad range of conditions contributing to social well-being, the spatial structure of cities appears to take on a somewhat different form. The limited evidence available suggests that the population of sub-areas of the city may be primarily differentiated according to the incidence of social problems rather than according to their socio-economic status, stage in life cycle, or ethnic background. If further studies of the kind reported here confirmed this, then the geographer's view of the city must change. He will begin to see patterns of social problems, or areal differentiation with respect to social well-being, transcending the economic and demographic patterns which have dominated his previous observations. He will thus achieve a more humanistic view of the internal differentiation of cities. He may then be led to examine the basic mechanism within the economic, political, and social system giving rise to such extreme disparities in the quality of life as exist in the American city, and to begin to design some alternatives to create a new spatial order.

REFERENCES CITED

Coughlin, R. E. (1970), *Goal Attainment Levels in 101 Metropolitan Areas*, Regional Science Research Institute, Discussion Paper No. 41, Philadelphia, Pa.

Dickinson, J. C., Gray, R. J. and Smith, D. M. (1972), "The Quality of Life in Gainesville, Florida: An Application of Territorial Social Indicators," *Southeastern Geographer*, 12.

Downey, G. T. and Hunt, R. G. (1972), "The Spatial Structure of Intraurban Criminal Behavior," paper presented at the Annual Meeting of the Association of American Geographers, Kansas City (mimeo).

Giggs, J. A. (1970), "Socially Disorganized Areas in Barry: A Multivariate Approach," in H. Carter and W. K. D. Davies, eds., *Urban Essays: Studies in the Geography of Wales*, Longmans, London, pp. 101-143.

Gray, R. J. (1972), *Social Well-being in Tampa: A Case Study in the Use of Social Indicators at the Intra-City Level*, unpublished MA thesis, Dept. of Geography, University of Florida.

Guertin, W. H. and Bailey, J. P. (1970), *Introduction to Modern Factor Analysis*, Edwards Bros. Inc., Ann Arbor, Mich.

Smith, D. M. and Gray, R. J. (1972), *Social Indicators for Tampa, Florida*, mimeo report, Urban Studies Bureau, University of Florida.

U.S. Department of Commerce, Bureau of the Census (1967), *Poverty Areas in the 100 Largest Metropolitan Areas*, Supplementary Report PC (S1)-54, *U.S. Census of Population*, USGPO, Washington, D.C.

CHAPTER 10

PROBLEMS AND
PROSPECTS

This book has argued for a new approach to the geographical study of man. It requires a broadening of our view of the human state, away from the current preoccupation with place in the economic system, to encompass the full range of conditions impinging on the quality of life. Social and cultural geographers have studied some such conditions for a long time and the profession in general is now extending its domain of concern. By setting the discussion here within the context of the contemporary interest in social indicators, this book has attempted to provide a specific conceptual focus for American geography's "revolution of social responsibility" with clear public policy implications.

In conclusion, some of the problems and opportunities arising from this approach may be examined briefly. If the emphasis in the discussion which follows seems to be on the difficulties that confront this kind of research and its application, it is because the merits of the concept of territorial social indicators as a way of structuring geographic knowledge should have emerged clearly in previous chapters. If the keynote is caution, it is because at times of intellectual uncertainty such as possess the field of geography today it is easy to be carried away by the superficial attraction of a new approach or technique, only later to discover its lack of depth or substance. There are, in fact, some important reservations to be made about the social indicators approach and these must be frankly recognized along with the exciting research opportunities the approach suggests.

Some Limitations of the Social Indicators Approach

A persistent theme in the literature on social indicators is that such measures can be of assistance in three different ways. These are (1) to establish and describe the state of society and how it is changing by

135

developing a system of "social accounts," (2) to evaluate the impact or effectiveness of specific programs, and (3) to provide a guide for public policy with respect to social goals and priorities. Chapter 5 examined these positions, and briefly discussed certain difficulties involved.

Recently, some of the more ambitious claims made initially on behalf of social indicators have been seriously challenged. Sheldon and Freeman (1970) argue that the development of social accounts is unreasonable in view of the lack of a social theory capable of defining the variables of a social system and the interrelationship between them, that the use of social indicators for project evaluation is presently impossible because of inability to control for contaminating variables, and that goals and priorities are more dependent on national objectives and values than on assembled data. Rivlin (1971, 59) echoes this last comment in expressing skepticism concerning the attention which politicians and policy makers are likely to give to cost-benefit analyses of social action programs. Sheldon and Freeman concede to social indicators the more modest and realistic goals of improving descriptive reporting, analysis of social change, and prediction of future social conditions. Land (1970) stresses the need to relate government expenditures to output variables via the organization of particular social institutions and redefines social indicators as the variables or parameters in models of such systems. Plessas and Fein (1972, 51) conclude a recent review of some differences within the social indicators movement with the hope that "future literature will include more data, more practical suggestions, more rigorous theoretical formulations and hypotheses with empirical import, and less meandering, unfocused verbosity."

It is somewhat in the spirit of this latter observation that the research treated in this book was embarked upon. While recognizing the limitations imposed by the conceptual and technical difficulties, an initial attempt has been made to develop some sets of territorial social indicators. These are offered as a descriptive device without any pretensions of providing great new insight into social processes, though some of the relationships observed are suggestive of cause and effect.

What is revealed by these studies is the extreme difficulty of even undertaking adequate geographical description given the present shortage of suitable data. Particularly serious is the reliance placed on aggregate data produced as a by-product of some administrative process and which at best constitutes only an indirect surrogate for the reality of human life experience which it purports to represent. At the end of Chapter 6 it was emphasized that individual well-being or social deprivation is a perceived relative state. As such it is measured most directly by survey research methods of the kind now being developed at the University of Michigan Institute for Social Research and the Berkeley Survey Research Center under large NSF social indicators research grants. Until projects of this kind bear fruit in the form of territorial indicators of perceived well-being the geographer must rely on the best available surrogates. As long as the defects of existing data are recognized and improvements are constantly sought a useful start can be made on describing some important dimensions of human existence conspicuously missing from the geographer's conventional view of the world. When attitudinal survey results are available they can be compared with the patterns suggested by existing data.

Social Accounting, Managerial Rationality, and Human Values

There are more fundamental problems involved in the social accounting approach than the development of sound numerical indicators, however. These concern such questions as whether we really need masses of new measures of the social state of the nation, whether this approach will really lead to improvements in the human condition where it is most desperately required, and whether we really want to live in a society rationally managed in pursuit of specific goals.

One of the dangers inherent in the social indicators movement is that precise measurement within a rigorous conceptual framework can become an end in itself. Compiling new sets of numbers provides members of the academic community with enormous scope for the exercise of intellectual dexterity, and the contemplation of statistics is less emotionally demanding (and less of a threat to job security) than direct social action. There is already a dispute within the social indicators movement between upholders of scientific rigor and those advocating a more activist approach (Plessas and Fein, 1972, 43-44).

The position taken here is that territorial social indicators should be developed within an action framework. Their development should arise from specific practical planning needs, as in the Tampa study, and their use should be guided by a philosophy dedicated to change and not to preservation of an unsatisfactory status quo. The information which they convey should also help to sensitize people to the magnitude of the spatial inequities within contemporary society. But most important of all, they should contribute to understanding. Good (1968, 7) has remarked that "there are ample statistics, forests of figures which, in their density, by their proliferating growth, suggest that compilation signifies progress and that we are getting somewhere. When the only place we really have got is deeper into the forest." The need is for better and useful figures, not for more of them—for some quality control and perhaps some pruning. And they need to be set within frameworks of understanding and action that will lead us out of the forest.

There is a feeling in some quarters that the development of further sets of social statistics will do no more than belabor the obvious. Harvey (1972b, 27) puts it as follows:

> We have enough information already and it is a waste of energy and resources to spend our time on such work. In fact, mapping even more evidence of man's patent inhumanity to man is counterrevolutionary in the sense that it allows the bleeding-heart liberal to pretend he is contributing to a solution when he in fact is not. This kind of empiricism is irrelevant.

The development of more and more precise social indicators in the face of such conspicuous problems as those which beset the American city may well be counter productive, if the objective really is to solve the problems.

It is difficult to avoid the logic of the comment by Rivlin (1971, 146) that "to do better, we must have a way of distinguishing better from worse" as the ultimate justification for the development of social indicators, but having distinguished better from worse we must have the will to do better.

This raises the next problem—that of how to determine what is better or worse. As was suggested in Chapter 5, there is a wide measure of agreement about desirable directions of change, but not about priorities. We know the signs to attach to an indicator but not the weights. As Rivlin (1971, 51) reminds us, to allocate scarce resources between alternative ends requires making choices such as whether it is better to cure cancer or to teach poor children to read. In the absence of cost-benefit ratios, in pecuniary or any other units, value judgements have to be made as to whether a cancer-free society with illiteracy is better or worse than a fully literate society with cancer. Of course, the choices are seldom framed as specifically as this. But financial resources are continually being allocated and re-allocated—between law enforcement and anti-poverty programs, between weapon systems and medical care—according to some prevailing social or political philosophy.

In an open democratic system, such choices should reflect the will of the people. But government in the United States seems unresponsive to the needs of the socially and economically deprived, while favoring resource allocations of benefit to large corporations and others who can bring special influence to bear on the political process. Used within such a system, a social accounting approach might do nothing more than strengthen the status quo. As Springer (1970, 13) puts it:

> . . .social indicators and reports are ideas whose time has come, because they are needed. What is required now is that they be developed with models of democracy as well as rational management, and rooted in a social science that has been developed to serve the needs of the poor, despised, and unorganized, as well as the rich and powerful.

Whether in the hands of the existing rich and powerful or of some Socialist bureaucracy supposedly more receptive to the wishes of the mass of the people, the managerial-rationality approach to social planning is bound to attract resentment and opposition. There is already some fear that societal goals may be set by a Big Brother or by an anonymous elite of "egghead" social engineers manipulating a dehumanized society from a computer console in Washington, D.C. The advocates of social system management often avoid the question of who actually decides what are desirable and undesirable system states, what is better or worse, and exactly what normative criteria the social indicators should measure. Perle (1970, 138) expresses some of these fears within the social indicators movement:

> The use of social knowledge for society control is an expression of managerial thinking. This view suggests that we can develop assessments of the societal order, predict our futures, and place social processes in a control theory setting. Though it may be possible to control some major activities of business firms (large or small) and even of government agencies, it is far less likely that we are or soon will be able to control complex social systems. This entire concept is completely elitist in attitude and frightening.

It is certainly not necessary to read George Orwell's *1984* to find some justification for this kind of suspicion in a society where the individual may be experiencing an increasing sense of powerlessness to influence a world organized by Big Government and Big Business.

Throughout the history of social and political philosophy there has been controversy between idealists and realists. The former are often cast as "utopians dedicated to the construction and imposition of abstract models, or blueprints, of the 'good society'," while the latter claim "a concrete sense of the actual, concerned, in varying degrees, with reforming it in the light of the possible" (Arblaster and Lukes, 1971, 2). Although the so-called realists can help the idealists to keep their feet on the ground, they have often in the past been merely preservers of the existing values threatened by what they depict as some impractical Utopian dream. As the debate on social planning continues, the idealists will have to face arguments from those who are philosophically in sympathy with them but doubtful about the practicality of social systems management, those who recognize the need for change but see important values like human freedom and dignity threatened by social planning, and those whose own interests depend in part on the existing chaos and therefore oppose any kind of change.

But the basic struggle is a political one. Whatever the problems of comprehensive social planning, the conclusion that the vast majority of the American people would gain from more rational planning of the (spatial) allocation of resources seems inescapable. Fundamental change in the provision and spatial organization of social services is required if the basic needs of all the people are to be met. The present disposition of power imposes severe political constraints on what can be achieved, both nationally and within the cities. In the American political arena, where pragmatism generally transcends ideals, it is probably more important to demonstrate that social planning has substantial support than that its consequences will be right, moral, or just.

Towards a Just Spatial Order

The geographer is a scholar, however, and not a political power broker. So what distinctive intellectual contribution can geography make in planning for the creation of a just society? Where is the crucial place of *territorial* social indicators? The answer was anticipated in the first chapter of this book in the discussion of the concept of social justice in spatial systems. First examined in detail by Harvey (1972a), this concept is now a subject of much interest within the geographical profession.

Territorial social indicators of the kind developed in previous chapters of this book portray an important yet often neglected dimension of the social system. They reveal the extent to which groups of people, defined by area of residence, have different experiences with respect to conditions that have a bearing on the well-being of society and the quality of individual life. They show that levels of income (broadly defined), environmental quality, health, education, social disorganization, alienation, and participation are subject to considerable variation between territories. There are extreme inequalities at all spatial levels.

But an inequable distribution is not necessarily unjust, whether it be between territories or between racial and ethnic groups. It depends on the criteria adopted. The existing gross inequalities in access to fee-for-service medical care, for example, and the consequent differences in the level of territorial health indicators might be justified if this service is regarded as a reward for labor compensated at market rates, though it is obviously unjust on the basis of other criteria such as need. Different criteria of distributive justice, if applied consistently, will lead to different spatial patterns of wealth, social services, and so on. The geographer wishing to judge a particular spatial distribution as just or unjust must have some norm or ideal as a basis for comparison. This involves accepting or taking a specific position with respect to the criteria which are or should be applied by society in distributing its benefits and exacting its penalties and deducing from this the just spatial order as a model against which to test reality. Then comes the task of identifying the mechanisms responsible for the disparity between reality and the just ideal, and applying this knowledge to the creation of an increasingly more just spatial order.

The geography of social well-being within the typical American city can serve as an illustration. The pattern observed in Tampa (Chapter 9) is typical, with a distinction between the socially-deprived core, the intermediate areas, and the affluent suburbs. If this is socially just, then it must be a consequence of properly high rewards for those entrepreneurs, managers, and professionals able to compete in a quasi-capitalist system largely organized by business, moderate rewards for the loyal and docile proletariat, and properly harsh penalties for those unable or unwilling (for whatever reason) to sell their labor or their souls. A rejection of these criteria in favor of merit, for example, might require much greater rewards for "success" in the hostile inner-city environment and less for those who entered the marketplace from a secure and achievement-oriented middle-class home. The criteria of need would clearly justify a much greater investment in social services in the ghetto compared with the suburbs, or the reverse of usual spatial allocations of resources. Public policy attempts to change the way things which have a bearing on the quality of life are distributed between groups of people and between territories.

In altering the geography of social well-being against the concept of territorial equity, a distinction must be made between the commitment of resources and the results achieved. Social indicators are conventionally output-oriented measures which reveal the results of the social system with respect to the condition in which people live. Thus to alter these conditions if they are deemed socially unjust requires either a change in inputs (i.e., investments) or a change in the system (i.e., reform of social institution) that transforms inputs into outputs. Ultimately it may require basic structural changes if the existing territorial social inequities within the American city are to be eliminated—changes possibly including public ownership of land, a reorganization of the learning and job training experience, and an elimination of free-enterprise medical care. But until the end is seen to be important enough to justify these means, the policy emphasis is likely to be on the reallocation of resources to equalize opportunity if not to fully compensate for past inequality.

Until very recently, territorial equality of opportunity was not part of the conventional rhetoric of American social justice. The observation by Mack (1970, 19) on "the need to correct inequalities in the educational opportunities available to Americans, regardless of race, color, or *region* [emphasis added]," cited in Chapter 1, was a rare departure from the usual reference to race, color, and creed. But a recent ruling by the California Supreme Court has called into question the propriety of some neighborhoods having better schools than others purely on the basis of the financial resources of their residents. The spatial equality of education is closely bound up with the busing issue and racial segregation by place of residence. In voting associated with the Florida Presidential Primary of March 1972, Governor Askew responded to an anti-busing question on the ballot by adding the following: "Do you favor providing an equal opportunity for quality education for all children regardless of race, creed, color, or *place of residence* [emphasis added] and oppose a return to a dual system of public schools?" The voters said Yes, four to one.

If the idea of territorial equality in educational opportunity has popular appeal, and if it is upheld by the courts, what are the implications for other services? As Rivlin (1971, 110) points out, "the courts are only beginning to come to grips with the problems raised by unequal distribution of publicly provided services." Yet differential access to such services has a major bearing on spatial variations in individual well-being, helping to maintain the "haves" in their privileged position of economic advantage and keeping the "have nots" in their place—in the cycle of poverty and social deprivation. If American society is able to see education not as a special case but representative of all social services, including those like medical care which are presently businesses, then it will be on the way to defining a new and distinctively geographical principle of social justice. This would be that people should not be discriminated against, with respect to means of access to the good life, by virtue of their location.

It is in giving substance to such an abstraction and in helping to see it realized that professional geography has a vital and revolutionary role to play in the creation of the new society.

The Revolution Required

It is one thing to propose a grand ideal, but quite another to achieve it. If there are grave injustices in the spatial structure of society, as is surely the case, detecting them is infinitely easier than correcting them. And it is not just a case of political constraints, important as they may be. A major academic problem is that our existing paradigms—the ways in which we conduct inquiry and structure knowledge—are unsatisfactory for prescriptive purposes. As Harvey (1972b) points out in his persuasive plea for a revolution in geographic thought, we have theories to account for ghetto formation but what society really needs is to eliminate the conditions that give rise to the truth of the theory. As the most profound of the classical location theorists said of economics, our real duty "is not to explain our sorry reality, but to improve it" (Lösch, 1954, 4). Geography places too much emphasis on describing and explaining our sorry reality and too little on improving it.

The approach developed in this book will be open to the same criticism if it fails to sensitize people to the extent of the spatial inequities and does not help to promote remedial action. Improvements in descriptive spatial social reporting are certainly required, and there is much constructive research still to be done in modeling the causal mechanisms responsible for our far from ideal reality. But somewhere there is a point of diminishing returns at which we must be prepared to back our hunches with real social reforms.

Some of the reforms that might be adopted to reduce America's spatial social problems are fairly obvious, and their effectiveness has already been demonstrated in other countries. If there are pockets of poverty and hunger, these can be eliminated by income transfers, industrial relocation, serious job training, and realistic minimum-wage laws. If there are areas with inadequate medical care facilities or people who cannot afford to use those which exist, this can be eliminated through a national health service. If there are inequities in other service provisions, these can be eliminated by instituting national standards and reallocating resources to achieve them. If there are blighted neighborhoods threatened by pollution, these can be reconstructed or protected by creative physical planning and strong development controls. If the race and class exclusiveness of suburbia is creating a polarized urban society, it can be broken by zoning laws and comprehensive metropolitan planning. And so on. All this is well within the capacity of the richest and most technically advanced people in the world.

What is lacking is not the programs and resources as much as the ability and willingness to implement them. While this may be largely attributed to the political power of vested interests threatened by social reform, some of the responsibility must rest with academics and planners. Paradoxically, the rigor and rationality that we are taught to bring to the job can be an impediment to social change. It can lead us to an exaggerated reverence for scientific method and technical sophistication and to a denigration of "qualitative" or "merely descriptive" work which may reflect a sharper intuitive alertness to the human condition than that of the quantitative and modeling schools. It can make us more interested in the computer program than in what goes in and what comes out. It supports the "new Philistinism" deplored by Gross (1966), in which all human affairs are reduced to dollars and cents in some gigantic and impeccably logical planning-programming-budgeting system. It leads us to seek optimal solutions where merely good ones will suffice. Like the programming models currently in fashion, we need to know when to stop iterating.

So the political struggle must be accompanied by some intellectual changes. As Buttimer (1972) eloquently puts it:

The structural reform which is needed in order to redress the glaring imbalance of power within society must be matched with an even more pervasive revolution within the minds and hearts of individual people. Structural reform and legislative social justice which is then meted out to hungry automatons so they may be lured into the "rational" folkways of middle-class society belongs to a Cartesian, managerial view of society. An appeal for internal renewal and creativity within the human individual implies an existential view of society, where people can create as well as accumulate, acquire as well as inherit, can learn to grapple with environmental problems rather than have them resolved for them by some intellectual or managerial elite.

In reviewing the geography of social well-being in the United States, and some of the problems raised, it is difficult to find a more persuasive concluding observation than that arrived at many years ago by Thorndike (1939, 67), in his pioneering study of the quality of urban life. He found that "cities are made better than others in this country primarily and chiefly by getting able and good people as residents. . . . Good people, rich or poor, earning much or earning little, are a good thing for a city." It takes good scholars to develop sound social indicators and effective social theory. It takes good technicians to translate this knowledge into social programs to correct the observed inequities, spatial or otherwise. But it takes good human beings to implement social reforms which will help others to realize their own perception of the good life. Good people in leadership positions may yet prove to be the most important of our scarce resources, for without them nothing will work.

REFERENCES CITED

Arblaster, A. and Lukes, S., eds. (1971), *The Good Society: A Book of Readings*, Methuen, London.

Buttimer, A. (1972), " 'Inequality,' 'Inefficiency,' and 'Spatial Injustice'," paper read at the Annual Meeting of the Association of American Geographers, Kansas City (mimeo).

Good, P. (1968), *The American Serfs: A Report on Poverty in the Rural South*, Ballantine Books, New York.

Gross, B. M. (1966), "The State of the Nation: Social Systems Accounting," in Bauer, ed. (1966), *Social Indicators*, pp. 154-271.

Harvey, D. (1972a), "Social Justice in Spatial Systems," in R. Peet, ed., *Geographical Perspectives on American Poverty*, Antipode Monographs in Social Geography, No. 1, Worcester, Mass., pp. 87-106.

_____ (1972b), "Revolutionary and Counter-revolutionary Theory in Geography and the Problem of Ghetto Formation," in *Perspectives in Geography*, Vol. II, Northern Illinois University Press, De Kalb (page references are to a mimeo version).

Land, K. C. (1970), "Social Indicators," in R. B. Smith, ed., *Social Science Methods*, The Free Press, New York.

Lösch, A. (1954), *The Economics of Location*, Yale University Press, New Haven, Conn.

Perle, E. D. (1970), "Editor's Introduction," *Urban Affairs Quarterly*, 6, No. 2, Special Issue on Urban Indicators, pp. 135-143.

Plessas, D. J. and Fein, R. (1972), "An Evaluation of Social Indicators," *Journal of the American Institute of Planners*, 38, No. 1, pp. 43-51.

Rivlin, A. M. (1971), *Systematic Thinking for Social Action*, The Brookings Institution, Washington, D.C.

Sheldon, E. B. and Freeman, H. B. (1970), "Notes on Social Indicators: Promises and Potential," *Policy Sciences*, 1, pp. 97-111.

Springer, M. (1970), "Social Indicators, Reports, and Accounts: Toward the Management of Society," *Annals of the American Academy of Political and Social Science*, 388, pp. 1-13.

Thorndike, E. L. (1939), *Your City*, Harcourt, Brace and Co., New York.